Death Hell and Gods Curse

ISBN 978-1-7330564-6-5 (Paper Back)
Book Design and Authorship by Don Pirozok
Editor Cheryl Pirozok

First Printing 2021 Amazon Publishing, United States

Published By: Pilgrims Progress Publishing
Spokane Valley WA. 99206
Website: www.donpirozok.com

Death Hell and Gods Curse

Section III
The Curse of God

Introduction

One of the reasons Christianity has suffered a decline in these last says is the lack of doctrinal understanding on life after death. So many non-Biblical beliefs have been incorporated into what happens after a person dies. As the result pagan concepts and philosophy have invaded the beliefs of many Christians about life after death. Classic doctrines like eternal judgment have been greatly altered. In many Christian camps the doctrine of Hell has been greatly compromised and, in some cases, has been almost eliminated.

Now days many persons simply believe, no matter what manner of evil or sin a person has lived no one goes to Hell, and every person is received into heaven. The judgment of God has all been but eliminated from many portions of the modern Church. So common has this belief become, even funerals are based upon the dead being in a far better place as each man is automatically forgiven upon death.

Many of the living speak of the joy they will experience when upon their deaths who will be reunited with their departed loved ones. The belief is no matter what kind of person upon death will unite their dead family members in heaven in a state of bliss.

However, this is not the Biblical narrative of life after death. In the first-place death is treated as an enemy in the Scriptures. Death is an unnatural state which has come as the result of mankind falling into sin. Also, death has horrible eternal consequences for the majority of the world's population. Death will not be the union and salvation into glory for the vast majority of humanity. The truth be told, for the vast majority of humanity will be outside of salvation. The Bible teaches men will die in their sins and go to Hell, not heaven. As sad and alarming as this might seem it is still the gospel truth.

If ever the Church comes back into teaching the doctrines of Christ teaching what is original sin, death, Hell, and the curse of God the fear of the Lord would come back into the household of faith. The consequences of sin and death must be faced by every man, woman, and child which will ever exist in this present evil age.
Before the return of Jesus Christ, men will age, and eventually die as the result of the corruption of sin and death. Only by faith in Christ is their redemption from sin and death. The dead will be resurrected at the Second Coming of Jesus Christ, each man in his order to stand in judgment before God.

God's way of saving us from sin and death required the incarnation, the death, burial, resurrection and ascension of the Son of God, Jesus Christ. In this way, Jesus Christ has the authority, and the ability to give eternal life to all who will call upon His name. The final acts of Christians individual salvation will be our own resurrection from the dead, and glorification into immortal bodies. Also, the Lord will redeem creation from all evidence of sin and death eliminating them completely. Renewing the world from corruption giving the redeemed a New Heavens and New Earth. World without sin.

For now, however, Christians must come to a biblical understanding of life after death and bring this clear message to a lost and dying world. Let us investigate together the doctrines of death, and life after death, and eternal salvation, or eternal judgment so as to give both hope, and warning to others. Let us not fall short of a deep understanding of Gods redemptive plan to deliver us from sin and death. Also, God's curse which came from the fall of man into sin. Let us shout out from the roof tops salvation from sin and death are found in Jesus Christ alone. For there is no other name given under heaven by which a man can be saved.

Section 1
What Is Death

Chapter 1
Understanding the Three Deaths

In the Bible three types of death are explained. A man who refuses Jesus Christ will experience all three. While a man who receives salvation, the forgiveness of sins, and the first resurrection will only experience two of the three. The first death is unavoidable for all of mankind, as it comes from the fall of man into original sin. God warned man not to disobey His command by partaking of the fruit of the knowledge of good and evil, "for the day you eat thereof you shall surely die." (Genesis 2:17)[1]

Original sin has generated spiritual death on the inside of everyman born into this world. A naturally born man, is born into original sin with a sin nature and is alienated from God at birth. A man born into original sin is a child of wrath by nature. Original sin has been passed upon every man and is what God warned would happen if man disobeyed His commandments. As the result of Adams disobedience to God death has passed to all

---

[1]

mankind. Men are born in sin with a sin nature dead to the life of God and are by nature are children of wrath. The only escape from spiritual death, the sin nature is to receive Jesus Christ as Lord, and be born again into a new life in Christ.

Romans 5:8-15[2]
8 But God commendeth his love toward us, in that, while we were yet sinners, Christ died for us.
9 Much more then, being now justified by his blood, we shall be saved from wrath through him.
10 For if, when we were enemies, we were reconciled to God by the death of his Son, much more, being reconciled, we shall be saved by his life.
11 And not only so, but we also joy in God through our Lord Jesus Christ, by whom we have now received the atonement.
12 Wherefore, as by one man sin entered into the world, and death by sin; and so death passed uponall men, for that all have sinned:
13 (For until the law sin was in the world: but sin is not imputed when there is no law.
14 Nevertheless death reigned from Adam to Moses, even over them that had not sinned after the similitude of Adam's transgression, who is the figure of him that was to come.
15 But not as the offence, so also is the free gift. For if through the offence of one many be

---

2

dead, much more the grace of God, and the
gift by grace, which is by
one man, Jesus Christ, abounded unto many.

The next death comes from original sin too. It is actual
death, the separation of the soul from the body, called
physical death. When a man dies physically the soul
separates out from the body, and then is appointed its
proper place awaiting the resurrection. For those who
die outside of salvation in Jesus Christ, their soul
descends into the underworld into Hell. The souls of a
righteous man also separates out of his body but does
not descend into Hell instead goes to the place of the
righteous dead called Paradise. Men like Abraham,
Isaac, and Jacob are in Paradise awaiting the first
resurrection. Where their souls will be reunited with
their bodies, and from that time will live in the immortal
state and can die no more.
However, those who do not qualify for the first
resurrection will continue to wait another 1000 years,
until the Second Resurrection. (Revelation 20:5-6) At
that time those who souls have been in Hell will be
raised from the dead joined to their bodies and judged
at the Great White Throne. Whosoever names are not
written in the Book of Life will be cast into the Lake of
Fire which is the final state of death.

The Lake of Fire is called the Second Death, as it occurs
after the dead are raised back into their bodies, and

then judged in their bodies and cast into the Lake of Fire. The final judgment is for all eternity with no hope of mercy, and without end. It is the final state of eternal punishment and torment which God will inflict upon the unrighteous man who names were not written in the Book of Life. For all those who are raised from the dead who names are written in the Book of Life, are raised into immortality, a glorified body and state. Upon the glorified saints the Second Death has no power, and they can die no more. The final state of the glorified saints is the New heavens and New Earth, where sin and death have been completely eliminated. Never again must an immortal man die or be judged for their sin. (Revelation 20:11-15)[3]

Sadly, history has proven more of humanity will die in their sins, and face the final judgment, the Lake of Fire. If the Church really believed in the Lake of Fire, the Second Death, Christians would be vigilant to warn fallen man to flee from the wrath to come. However, we are in a day where inside the Church to preach Hell fire has become politically incorrect. Instead, men will only say the love of God saves you, and some are even saying there is no Hell. Falsely teaching in the end all men will be saved, no matter how they lived their lives before death. Many in the modern Church have fallen to this kind of deception. These false doctrines make fallen man comfortable in their sin making their path to Hell the Broadway to destruction.

From the three deaths overview we can see death is connected to the fall of humanity into original sin. Since all who derive their natural human life from Adam have been given the sin nature, all mankind must face death. Sin and death are instrumentally connected by nature. You had no choice over your fallen nature, it is the fact of fallen life. You have by nature been born in sin, a natural enemy to God by nature a child of Gods wrath. You are not by nature one who will naturally seek out God and obey Him living for His will alone. Instead, you will be naturally rebellious and seek your own will and way refusing the will of God for your life. No matter how good one person might appear in comparison to another person, in comparison to God there is no one good not even one. There is no one who seeks after God, however many will incorporate religion into their beliefs about God. Religion does not change the fact your sin nature has alienated you from God, and you do not naturally have Christs life. Instead, You are born into this world with spiritual death one the inside.

Romans 3:9-18[4]
9 What then? are we better than they? No, in no wise: for we have before proved both Jews and Gentiles, that they are all under sin.
10 As it is written, there is none righteous, no, not one:
11 There is none that understandeth, there is none that seeketh after God.

---

[4]

12 They are all gone out of the way, they are together become unprofitable; there is none that doeth good, no, not one.
13 Their throat is an open sepulchre; with their tongues they have used deceit; the poison of asps is under their lips:
14 Whose mouth is full of cursing and bitterness:
15 Their feet are swift to shed blood:
16 Destruction and misery are in their ways:
17 And the way of peace have they not known:
18 There is no fear of God before their eyes.

From being born spiritually dead alienated from the life of God, everyone will live a life of sin breaking the laws of God living under Gods wrath. Upon death, an actual separation of soul and body will manifest as a dead man becomes a disembodied soul. The soul must go to its appointed place according to Gods curse and judgment. If unredeemed the disembodied soul will descend into Hell and suffer the judgment of Hell fire. If redeemed the disembodied soul will also descend, but not into torment instead into the place of the redeemed called Paradise. Upon the death of Jesus Christ, His soul separated out of His body, and descended into the earth into Paradise the place of the righteous dead.

Acts 2:22-32[5]
22 Ye men of Israel, hear these words; Jesus of Nazareth, a

5

man approved of God among you bymiracles and wond
ers and signs, which God did by him in the midst of
you, as ye yourselves also know:
23 Him, being delivered by
the determinate counsel and foreknowledge of God, ye
have taken, and by wicked hands have crucified and
slain:
24 Whom God hath raised up, having loosed the
pains of death: because it was not possible that he
should be holden of it.
25 For David speaketh concerning him, I foresaw the
Lord always before my face, for he is on my right, that I
should not be moved:
26 Therefore did my heart rejoice, and my tongue was
glad; moreover also my flesh shall rest in hope:
27 Because thou
wilt not leave my soul in hell, neither wilt thou
suffer thine Holy One see corruption.
28 Thou hast made known to me the ways of life; thou
shalt make me full of joy with thy countenance.
29 Men and brethren, let me freely speak unto you of th
e patriarch David, that he
is both dead andburied, and his sepulchre is with us unt
o this day.
30 Therefore being a
prophet, and knowing that God had sworn with an
oath to him, that of the fruit of his loins, according
to the flesh, he would raise up Christ to
sit on his throne;
31 He seeing this before spake of the resurrection of

Christ, that his soul was not left in hell, neither
his flesh did see corruption.
32 This Jesus hath God raised
up, whereof we all are witnesses.

The most technical form of death recognized by all
humans is when the physical makes up of man ceases to
function and sustain the man's life. When the body by
reason of sickness, accident, injury, or old age, can no
longer sustain life the body will cease to function. Since
the human soul and spirit require a healthy physical
body in order to exist in this physical world, death then
is the bodies inability to sustain life. However, when the
body no longer can sustain life, the person does not go
into a state of nonexistence. Instead, the persons soul
separates out of their body, and now that individual will
exist in the state of death, a disembodied human soul.

The state of death is not cessation of life, or
nonexistence, or even the annihilation of the souls. All
these beliefs are non-Christian developed by human
theory, or philosophical beliefs which come from other
religions. Now days even in the Church, doctrines have
arisen which pervert the truth of life after death. For
example, the lie, at death a soul is burned out of
existence annihilated by God never to exist again. This is
a completely false doctrine, as the Scriptures prove the
soul of mankind to be eternal. Once in existence the
souls of the dead will be reunited to their bodies at the
Second Coming of Jesus Christ. After which, the state of

their eternity is determined either in the New Heavens and New Earth, or the Lake of Fire.

There is no other way God will deal with the eternal soul, except by reuniting the dead to their bodies for the rest of eternity. The plan of God is the resurrection of the dead with disembodied souls back into their bodies for eternal judgment. Both the righteous and the wicked are resurrected, however the final states are different with the wicked suffering for all eternity in the Lake of Fire.

Chapter Two
Where Do Men Go When They Die

The religious belief that all men who die go to heaven is not from the Bible, neither is it a part of the doctrinal beliefs of the early Church. In the time of Christ, the Jews believed upon death the soul of all men descended into the underworld. Both the righteous and the wicked were appointed places for their disembodied souls awaiting their lot in the resurrections out from among the dead. Jesus Christ maintained the Jewish belief by stating upon His death, His soul would descend into Paradise. Sometimes called Abrahams Bosom, Paradise is the place agreed upon by proper Bible teaching where the disembodied soul of Jesus Christ descended. So, until the time of Christ, the souls of men descended into the underworld into the places of the departed dead, Paradise, or Hell.

This might be surprising to many Christians who have been taught their whole lives death means going into heaven. However, the Scriptures are clear Paradise was or is still in the heart of the earth, and not up into the realms of Heaven.

Acts 2:24-32[6]
24 Whom God hath raised up, having loosed the pains of death: because it was not possible that he should be holden of it.
25 For David speaketh concerning him, I foresaw the Lord always before my face, for he is on my right hand, that I should not be moved:
26 Therefore did my heart rejoice, and my tongue was glad; moreover, also my flesh shall rest in hope:
27 Because thou wilt not leave my soul in hell, neither wilt thou suffer thine Holy One to see corruption.
28 Thou hast made known to me the ways of life; thou shalt make me full of joy with thy countenance.
29 Men and brethren let me freely speak unto you of the patriarch David, that he is both dead and buried, and his sepulchre is with us unto this day.
30 Therefore being a prophet and knowing that God had sworn with an oath to him, that of the fruit of his loins, according to the flesh, he would raise up Christ to sit on his throne.
31 He seeing this before spake of the resurrection of Christ, that his soul was not left in hell, neither his flesh did see corruption.
32 This Jesus hath God raised up, whereof we all are witnesses.

6

Jesus Christ was raised up from the portion of the underworld called Paradise, where His disembodied soul did not see corruption. Jesus Christ was in fact in the state of death being separated out of His body for three days. Upon the third day the soul of Christ was raised up from among the righteous dead and reunited with His body which had been wrapped and laid in the Tomb.

Upon meeting Mary Magdalene at the Tomb, Jesus Christ affirmed He had not yet ascended into Heaven. (John 20:17) Instead had only been raised up from among the dead into His resurrected body. A rejoining of soul and body, a newly resurrected man up from among the dead. The soul of Jesus Christ did not see corruption in Hell like the unrighteous dead man instead was joined with the righteous dead in Paradise. Upon resurrection Christ raised up from among the righteous dead, the first born from the dead.

The Greek word rendered Hell in Acts 2:27&31 is actually the word Hades. Which can give us some insight into the underworld. At the time of the death of Jesus Christ went into Hades which is the overall description given to the underworld. Hades then would consist both of Paradise and Hell.
Also, the Scriptures informs us of another section of the underworld different from Paradise, or Hell, a place called Tartarus. The place which God chained up the

angels who left their first estate by violating Gods laws in illegal interaction with human beings in the Days of Noah. These fallen angels are now chained up in Tartarus, another part of the underworld. So, Hades would consist of at least three distinct underworld places where spiritual beings exist. Paradise the place of the righteous dead, Hell for the unrighteous dead, and Tartarus the place of judgment for a specific class of angels judged by God.

2 Peter 2:4-9[7]
4 For if God spared not the angels that sinned, but cast them down to hell, and delivered them into chains of darkness, to be reserved unto judgment.
5 And spared not the old world, but saved Noah the eighth person, a preacher of righteousness, bringing in the flood upon the world of the ungodly.
6 And turning the cities of Sodom and Gomorrha into ashes condemned them with an overthrow, making them an ensample unto those that after should live ungodly.
7 And delivered just Lot, vexed with the filthy conversation of the wicked:
8 (For that righteous man dwelling among them, in seeing and hearing, vexed his righteous soul from day to day with their unlawful deeds;)
9 The Lord knoweth how to deliver the godly out of temptations, and to reserve the unjust unto the day of judgment to be punished:

---

[7]

Now it is obvious until the time of Christ mankind upon their deaths did not ascend into heaven like beliefs held today. Instead, all men upon death had their souls descend into the underworld, into Hades the place of the dead, both of the righteous and wicked. So, when did the belief change? The belief men ascended into to heaven upon death and enter the glorified state immediately. When did this change first come about?

"The earliest of the Apostolic Fathers Clement of Rome does not mention entry into heaven after death but instead expresses belief in the Resurrection of the Dead after a period of "slumber"[5] at the Second Coming.[6] A fragment from the early 2nd century of one of the lost volumes of Papias, a Christian bishop, expounds that "heaven" was separated into three distinct layers. He referred to the first as just "heaven", the second as "paradise", and the third as "the city". Papias taught that "there is this distinction between the habitation of those who produce a hundredfold, and that of those who produce sixty-fold, and that of those who produce thirty-fold".[7]
According to some views, some Christians in the 1st century believed that the Kingdom of God was coming to earth within their own lifetimes.[3] They looked forward to a divine future on earth.[3] When the Kingdom of God did not arrive, according to this hypothesis, championed by Bart Ehrman (2006), Christians gradually refined their hopes so that they

came to look forward to an immediate reward in heaven after death, rather than to a future divine kingdom on earth[3]—despite the churches' continuing to use the major creeds' statements of belief in a coming Resurrection Day and World to Come.
In the 2nd century AD, Irenaeus (a Greek bishop) wrote that not all who are saved would merit an abode in heaven itself.[8]" (Wikipedia)[8]

Let us look at some facts. The Scriptures teach paradise the place of the righteous dead was part of Hades. Upon death for thousands of years the righteous descended into the earth, into Paradise where they awaited their resurrection out from among the dead. So, for thousands of years the righteous dead were in the underworld not heaven. Next upon the death of Jesus Christ His soul departed into Paradise into the underworld for three days. Then upon the third day was raised up from among the dead back into His body. Proof Jesus Christ has yet to ascend was after the resurrection told Mary Magdalene He had not yet ascended into Heaven. It is not until the fortieth day after the resurrection, the Bible says Jesus Christ then ascended into Heaven.

Now many Church fathers insisted hundreds of years after the resurrection of Jesus Christ, the righteous dead still descended into Paradise awaiting their resurrection. Where the Jewish Church fathers wrong, or the early

Church fathers of the first two centuries? Had Jesus Christ removed Paradise from the underworld into Heaven when He was raised from the dead?

When did the shift actually happen? When did the Church began to teach the saints enter glory immediately upon death? To go into heaven as a disembodied soul, and from there the place of Heavens glory await the resurrection? Surprisingly, the answer lies with the formation of Catholicism. New beliefs about death and the underworld comes from Catholic doctrine which were never before introduced into Judo Christian doctrine. The first is Purgatory, a Catholic intermediate state of the underworld, a place of purification to qualify for salvation. The Second is entrance as a disembodied spirit into glory immediately upon death.

What is Purgatory

"In addition to accepting the states of heaven and hell, Catholicism envisages a third state before being admitted to heaven. According to Catholic doctrine, some souls are not sufficiently free from the temporal effects of sin and its consequences to enter the state of heaven immediately, nor are they so sinful and hateful of Christ as to be destined for hell either.[29] Such souls, ultimately destined to be united with God in heaven, must first be cleansed through purgatory – a state of purification.[30] Through purgatory, souls "achieve the holiness necessary to enter the joy of heaven."[31] The Church makes a distinction between mortal sin, which incurs both temporal punishment and eternal punishment, and venial sin, which incurs only temporal punishment.[32] Mortal sin is a "sin whose object is grave matter and which is also committed with full knowledge and deliberate consent."[32] "If it is not redeemed by repentance and God's forgiveness, it causes exclusion from Christ's kingdom and the eternal death of hell, for our freedom has the power to make choices for ever, with no turning back."[32] (Wikipedia)[9]

Is Purgatory Biblical? Do men have a second chance with God after death? Will the purging fires of an intermediate state after death purify the soul so a man can be cleansed from his sins not cleansed in this life? Can a soul of a man not qualified for heaven, then be purged by the fires of God, and pay for his entrance into heaven? Can men pay indulgences for souls in Purgatory, as a means to pay their sin debut to God?

All these beliefs together sum up the doctrine of Purgatory which cannot be found in the doctrines of the Bible. Salvation is obtained through grace and faith in Jesus Christ before man's death. After death, each is appointed their proper abode, Hell, or Paradise, awaiting their resurrection. The idea man can attain to heaven was first introduced by Catholicism. The progression from the underworld by human attainment came in degrees eventually earning the right to ascend

---

into heaven. These doctrines are an invention of Roman Catholicism.

In Christian orthodoxy, Jesus suffered for our sins so that we could be delivered from Hell. To say that we must also suffer for our sins is to say that Jesus' suffering was insufficient. To say that we must atone for our sins by cleansing in Purgatory is to deny the sufficiency of the atoning sacrifice of Jesus. The idea that we have to suffer for our sins after death is contrary to everything the Bible says about salvation.

Now this does not eliminate the fact Christians will be judged at the Second Coming of Jesus Christ and the Judgment Seat of Christ? Scriptural passages which Catholics say justify evidence of Purgatory, like 1 Corinthians 3:15, which says, "If it is burned up, he will suffer loss; he himself will be saved, but only as one escaping through the flames." However, this passage refers to the Judgment Seat of Christ, and the Second Coming not to an intermediate state to save men at death. All Christians will pass through the judicial fires of I Corinthians 3 to test the quality of every man's works. Not to purge venial sins, so as to be saved for heaven. The loss written in this passage is one of rewards, not of salvation as the fire can burn away all the defective material, while the Christians salvation remains intact. The mixture of Purgatory with the judicial fire of God has perverted the doctrine of eternal judgment.

1 Corinthians 3:10-15[10]

10 According to the grace of God, which is given unto me, as a wise master builder, I have laid the foundation, and another buildeth thereon. But let every man take heed how he buildeth thereupon.

11 For other foundation can no man lay than that is laid, which is Jesus Christ.

12 Now if any man build upon this foundation gold, silver, precious stones, wood, hay, stubble;

13 Every man's work shall be made manifest: for the day shall declare it, because it shall be revealed by fire; and the fire shall try every man's work of what sort it is.

14 If any man's work abide which he hath built thereupon, he shall receive a reward.

15 If any man's work shall be burned, he shall suffer loss: but he himself shall be saved; yet so as by fire.

The loses which the fires of judgment reveal are based upon works after coming into saving faith. They are not an intermediate state, or loss of salvation. The men judged are all saints, no unrighteous will stand at the judgment Seat of Christ. Loss at the Judgment Seat of rewards can be very grievous indeed, but do not determine our eternal salvation. For the Cross of Jesus Christ has already bought and paid for the saint's eternal salvation.

---

[10]

The very idea of Purgatory and human merit which accompany it are a failure to affirm the Cross as the only means to pay the price for mankind's sin. Prayer for the dead, indulgences, meritorious works on behalf of the dead, fail to recognize that Jesus' death was sufficient to pay the penalty for all of our sins. Jesus Christ alone is the atoning sacrifice for our sins there is no other way for sin to be forgiven. Purgatory attacks Christ's work of atonement by limiting His sacrifice to atoning for original sin or sins committed before salvation.

Purgatory and human merit then makes a demand for a person to pay for their own sin. If we must in order to be saved pay for, atone for, or suffer because of our sins, then Jesus' death was not a perfect or complete, and sufficient sacrifice. Purgatory is understood by Catholics as a place of cleansing in preparation for heaven because they do not recognize by Jesus' sacrifice we are already cleansed, and declared righteous, forgiven, redeemed, reconciled, and sanctified.

Now we can see how Catholicism began to grant rewards and judgments based upon human merit, and not the work of the Cross. It seems the Catholic Church wanted to claim control over a person's eternal state by forming doctrines like Purgatory. In this way, the Catholic Church becomes the agent of salvation, not the Cross of Jesus Christ. To grant a man salvation after death apart from the Cross, and reward immediate access into heaven without resurrection is a Catholic invention. However, like many other religious perversions, those false doctrines often become the main beliefs of society. For a long time, the Catholic Church has granted Catholics access to Gods glory upon death if in good standing with the Catholic Church. No need to wait for a future resurrection instead the saints who are saved by priestly sacraments were given the glorified position. An entrance into heaven immediate upon death.

The Assumption of Virgin Mary
The whole doctrine of Catholics attaining to heaven before the resurrection is also further fostered by the Assumption of Mary.

"The Catholic Church teaches as dogma that the Virgin Mary "having completed the course of her earthly life, was assumed body and soul into heavenly glory".[5] This doctrine was dogmatically defined by Pope Pius XII on 1 November 1950, in the apostolic constitution Munificentissimus Deus by exercising papal infallibility.[6] While the Catholic Church and Eastern Orthodox Church believe in the Dormition of the Theotokos, which is the same as the Assumption,[7] whether Mary had a physical death has not been dogmatically defined." (Wikipedia)[11]

11

For centuries, the false doctrine the Virgin Mary was assumed into heaven, like Jesus Christ, both in soul and body has been taught by Catholicism. Once again Christians should take note how far removed from orthodoxy is the Assumption of Mary. The idea of glorification upon death is promoted instead of standing in judgment at the end of the age, and the resurrection out from among the dead. Glorification by Catholicism has over the years eroded the fact that death is an enemy yet to be conquered at the Second Coming. Instead, the conquest of death and the glorification of the saints is apart from the bodily resurrection of the dead. In Mary's case however, the glorified state to which Mary has attained is already soul and body. Apparently, Mary is a coredeemer, with Jesus Christ, a fourth person in the Godhead equal to Jesus Christ.

What does all this error and human tradition point out? Many false doctrines have replaced Biblical facts when it comes to beliefs of life after death. Catholicism over time eroded the need of resurrection before glorification. If you were a Catholic in good standing with the Church, the promise of heaven was given by the Catholic Church. Celebrations like included in Lent prove the doctrines of Catholicism have joined with pagan religions rewarding the faithful with heavens glory.

The Celebration of Lent

"The fourth Sunday of Lent sees the commemoration of Saint John Climacus, the sixth century Abbott of St. Katherines Monastery on Sinai who wrote "The Ladder of Divine Descent Ascent." He is seen as the great exemplar of the ascetic life, and in manuscripts and icons the ladder of ascent has often been illustrated. A famous late twentieth century icon at the Monastery of St Katherine shows the ladder stretching up from earth to heaven; monks make the ascent assisted by prayers of the community of the saints, but some are being attacked and dragged off the ladder by a variety of demons. Saint John Climacus leads the ascent and is welcomed into heaven by Christ; the ladder has 30 rungs in keeping with the 30 stages of the monastic ascent. The liturgical texts for this Sunday use the Parable of the Good Samaritan with much eloquence and urgency."

Festival icons for the Christian year by John Baggley 2000 ISBN 0-88141-201-5 pages 83-84 [1][12]

Although he had a lot of heretical views, Justin Martyr (considered to be a saint by both Catholics and Protestants, but not by those of us in the Church of God) in the second century wrote:

"For I choose to follow not men or men's doctrines, but God and the doctrines [delivered] by Him. For if you have fallen in with some who are called Christians, but

---

[12]

who do not admit this [truth], and venture to blaspheme the God of Abraham, and the God of Isaac, and the God of Jacob; who say there is no resurrection of the dead, and that their souls, when they die, are taken to heaven; do not imagine that they are Christians".
(Justin. Dialogue with Trypho. Chapter 80).[13]

This differs from the official Catechism of the Catholic Church:
Those who die in God's grace and friendship and are perfectly purified live forever with Christ. They are like God for ever, for they "see him as he is," face to face:

"By virtue of our apostolic authority, we define the following: According to the general disposition of God, the souls of all the saints . . . and other faithful who died after receiving Christ's holy Baptism (provided they were not in need of purification when they died, . . . or, if they then did need or will need some purification, when they have been purified after death, . . .) already before they take up their bodies again and before the general judgment - and this since the Ascension of our Lord and Savior Jesus Christ into heaven - have been, are and will be in heaven, in the heavenly Kingdom and celestial paradise with Christ, joined to the company of the holy angels. Since the Passion and death of our Lord Jesus Christ, these souls have seen and do see the divine

---

13

essence with an intuitive vision, and even face to face, without the mediation of any creature.

Thus, a Catholic saint is teaching that those who hold the current Catholic view are not Christian. Catholics either do not seem to know of the contradiction here or dismiss it. But the reality is that early professors of Christ did not teach that upon death one went to heaven in a conscious manner."
Co-writer.com/heaven.htm[14]

Chapter 3
What Is Resurrection

Before a man can be glorified into immortality the Bible says he must be delivered out from the state of death. The Scriptures do not recognize a man entering into the glorified state until the Second Coming and the resurrection out from among the dead. The only resurrected glorified man according to Scriptures is Jesus Christ, the first born from the dead. So significant to Christian salvation is the resurrection, the Scriptures actually appoint a day, the Day of Redemption as the future salvation of our bodies.

Romans 8:18-23[15]
18 For I reckon that the sufferings of this present time are not worthy to be compared with the glory which shall be revealed in us.

---

[14]

[15]

19 For the earnest expectation of the creature waiteth for the manifestation of the sons of God.

20 For the creature was made subject to vanity, not willingly, but by reason of him who hath subjected the same in hope,

21 Because the creature itself also shall be delivered from the bondage of corruption into the glorious liberty of the children of God.

22 For we know that the whole creation groaneth and travaileth in pain together until now.

23 And not only they, but ourselves also, which have the first fruits of the Spirit, even we ourselves groan within ourselves, waiting for the adoption, to wit, the redemption of our body.

24 For we are saved by hope: but hope that is seen is not hope: for what a man seeth, why doth he yet hope for?

25 But if we hope for that we see not, then do we with patience wait for it.

If we take from this passage fallen creation being restored at the Second Coming and Day of Redemption. In which all the effects of sin, death and corruption will be put away with death being the final enemy. Paul is saying the creation groans, we who are in our mortal bodies, and those who are in a disembodied state are longing for their deliverance from mortality. For the creation is waiting for the day of revealing when Gods sons are made manifest in the first resurrection. Could not part of God's creation who are longing for those days, also be the righteous dead saints? Is the vanity to which our original creation been made subject, the disembodied state of death? Even those who are alive in their mortal bodies desire not to be unclothed (death), by clothed upon by immortality. Now the righteous dead saints will be delivered from the bondage of corruption, (state of death), into the glorious liberty of the children of God (resurrection).

Creation who travels together, includes those who are alive now in their mortal bodies (alive in Christ), groan and travails in pain (pains of sin and death) until now (awaiting our redeemed bodies). Paul makes it clear the redemption we are in travail with is the redemption of our bodies. Resurrection is Biblically accurate, proving redemption and glorification of the saints is future. Not based upon the day we die, instead on the day we are raised from the dead. By hope in the future resurrection are the saints patiently waiting for it, both the dead in Christ, and the living.(Some who are alive at Christ's coming will be taken alive into the air, not suffering physical death.)

So, the challenge is not to put glorification and the saint's redemption at their death by placing them as disembodied souls in heaven now. As formerly stated for thousands of years deliverance was thought to be the saints raised up from the earth as the Second Coming of the Lord. Up from the dust of the earth and out from their graves. Not down with the Lord, and then back into their bodies.

Resurrection is clearly attached to our redemption and can only occur at the Second Coming of the Lord. It would be wrong to say when Christians die, then are immediately raised from the dead into their immortal glorified bodies. It is equally wrong to have believed when the Old Testament saints died, they were immediately taken into heaven as disembodied souls.

So, would Jesus Christ who now has been raised from the dead take disembodied souls of Christians into heaven to await the resurrection? In the past the place of the righteous dead was clearly Paradise, not heaven. Instead, a place made for the disembodied souls in the underworld. Yet, a lovely place, a garden like place for the righteous dead.

The only question which truly remains; has Paradise been removed from the underworld into heaven? The body of evidence is resurrection up put from out among the dead, instead of down from the angels. However, one should examine the question more throughly, as some Christian teachers point to New Testament Scriptures to teach Paradise has in fact been removed to heaven. At this point I will leave the debate here so as to see other important factors which will help us determine the state of death, and our eternal estate.

I want to bring into remembrance the Scriptures teach two resurrections not just one. The first resurrection is for the righteous only, separated by 1000 years before the rest of the dead will be raised. Here is some Scriptural evidence which demonstrates these facts.

Revelation 20:1-6[16]

1 And I saw an angel come down from heaven, having the key of the bottomless pit and a great chain in his hand.

2 And he laid hold on the dragon, that old serpent, which is the Devil, and Satan, and bound him a thousand years,

3 And cast him into the bottomless pit, and shut him up, and set a seal upon him, that he should deceive the nations no more, till the thousand years should be fulfilled: and after that he must be loosed a little season.

4 And I saw thrones, and they sat upon them, and judgment was given unto them: and I saw the souls of them that were beheaded for the witness of Jesus, and for the word of God, and which had not worshipped the beast, neither his image, neither had received his mark upon their foreheads, or in their hands; and they lived and reigned with Christ a thousand years.

5 But the rest of the dead lived not again until the thousand years were finished. This is the first resurrection.

16

6 Blessed and holy is he that hath part in the first resurrection: on such the second death hath no power, but they shall be priests of God and of Christ and shall reign with him a thousand years.

From Scriptures we can see two resurrections which are connected to the Second Coming of Jesus Christ. The first resurrection coincides with the end of this age, and the gathering together of the saints in the clouds. With the dead in Christ raised first then those Christians who are alive and remain will be caught up also. The connection of the first resurrection and the second Coming, and the end of this present evil age are all interconnected. The first resurrection qualifies the saints for entrance into the Kingdom age, which is the one thousand years rule of Jesus Christ on earth.

The Scriptures teach blessed and holy are they who have part in the first resurrection, as they are raised into immortality, and can die no more. Upon the first resurrection saints, the Second Death has no power. Instead, the first resurrection saints are as the angels of heaven, and reign with Jesus Christ as kings and priests in the Millennial Kingdom.

However, the rest of the dead will not be raised back into their bodies until the one-thousand-year kingdom of heaven has been completed. Those who will be raised in the Second Resurrection are men who are unrighteous, and most have been resigned to Hell. The

Second Resurrection does have some men who names were written in the Book of Life, and are granted the New Heavens and New Earth, even though they were not qualified for the Kingdom age. The Second Resurrection is also the last resurrection and will finalize the state of eternity for every man. Those who do not have their names written in the Book of Life will be judged according to their works at the Great White Throne. They have been raised back into their bodies, delivered from Hell, and then cast body and soul into the Lake of Fire the eternal flames and suffering of the wicked. This second resurrection is also called the Second Death, as it occurs after the body has been raised back to life, and then judged to the Lake of Fire.

Revelation 20:11-15[17]
11 And I saw a great white throne, and him that sat on it, from whose face the earth and the heaven fled away; and there was found no place for them.
12 And I saw the dead, small and great, stand before God; and the books were opened: and another book was opened, which is the book of life: and the dead were judged out of those things which were written in the books, according to their works.
13 And the sea gave up the dead which were in it; and death and hell delivered up the dead which were in them: and they were judged every man according to their works.

_____

[17]

14 And death and hell were cast into the lake of fire. This is the second death.
15 And whosoever was not found written in the book of life was cast into the lake of fire.

Now that we see the Biblical way for men to be delivered from the power of sin and death is by resurrection. The Word of God demonstrates resurrection is up from the dead, and up from the earth from out among the dead in the underworld. Now very little argument comes about the unrighteous dead whose abode is in Hell. Whose judgment continues in Hell until their judgment at the Great White Throne. The debate begins over the righteous dead, and their existence in heaven today. If we eliminate the development of the doctrine of Catholicism wrongly teaching being glorified upon death, with the saints immediately admitted access into Heaven. Then we must consider the possibility, the righteous dead are in the underworld too. The portion of Hades called Paradise in the underworld apart from Hell. Many will be raised up from the earth (Paradise) in the first resurrection.

The apostle Paul also weighs in by calling the first resurrection a prize, a high calling which he was striving to attain. The cost of the first resurrection would require Paul to count everything loss, and to be conformed to the fellowship of Christs sufferings. Paul said he would conform to the death of Christ, lest by any means Paul could attain to the resurrection of the dead. Why would the apostle Paul teach he was trying to attain the resurrection of the dead where most Christians of today simply assume it was already given by the Cross? Is it possible the prize of the high calling, is the first of two resurrections, and must be attained by righteous conduct and living after coming to saving faith by grace?

Paul said not that I have attained already the out resurrection, (first resurrection) where Paul wanted to win the prize of being raised with qualified saints first. The Bible teaches all men will be raised back into their bodies, however, only the qualified will be raised out from among the dead first. Paul said, he had not yet attained, but forgetting those things which were behind he pressed towards the prize of the high calling qualifying for the first resurrection. The cost of the first resurrection is righteous holy living, to count all things loss in qualification of the prize of resurrection reward. Paul said, every man in Christ should have this same attitude of pressing for the prize. The reward of the righteous, the first resurrection.

In this way some will be raised up first before others, out from the rest of the dead. Paul's passages confirm what John wrote in the twentieth chapter of Revelation. The righteous dead in Christ who qualify for the first resurrection are raised at the end of this age. They reign with Christ in the millennial kingdom for one thousand years and are immortal who can die no more. After the Kingdom age comes the Second Resurrection, the Great White Throne Judgment where each man is judged according to their works. Some who did not qualify for the first resurrection whose names are written in the Book of Life are then raised from the dead. Even though disqualified from the first resurrection are given the New Heaven and New Earth, and immortal glorified bodies. This then is the order of the resurrection, both of the righteous, and unrighteous.

Philippians 3:8-15[18]
8 Yea doubtless, and I count all things but loss for the excellency of the knowledge of Christ Jesus my Lord: for whom I have suffered the loss of all things, and do count them but dung, that I may win Christ,
9 And be found in him, not having mine own righteousness, which is of the law, but that which is through the faith of Christ, the righteousness which is of God by faith:
10 That I may know him, and the power of his resurrection, and the fellowship of his sufferings, being made conformable unto his death.
11 If by any means I might attain unto the resurrection of the dead.
12 Not as though I had already attained, either were already perfect: but I follow after, if that I may apprehend that for which also, I am apprehended of Christ Jesus.

18

13 Brethren, I count not myself to have apprehended: but this one thing I do, forgetting those things which are behind, and reaching forth unto those things which are before,

14 I press toward the mark for the prize of the high calling of God in Christ Jesus.

15 Let us therefore, as many as be perfect, be thus minded: and if in anything ye be otherwise minded, God shall reveal even this unto you.

"The being raised in the first resurrection assures a place in the [millennial] kingdom, and honour therein; and such as are not then raised will miss that kingly glory, since the second and last resurrection is not to take place till after the millennial period (Rev. 20: 4-6). On the other hand, those who attain to that kingship will retain it forever, and not cease to reign at the end of the thousand years, for it is written concerning such that "they shall reign for ever and ever" (Rev. 22: 5). From which it would appear that those who enter the [eternal] kingdom [in 'a new heaven and a new earth' (Rev. 21: 1)] at the close of the millennial period will not attain to kingly dignity therein, since that is stated only of those who had reached the bridal glory, the members of the Jerusalem which is above. It thus becomes a matter of everlasting consequence to be of those who participate in the first resurrection.

The phrase "the out resurrection from among the dead" (teen exanastasin teen ek nekron) is an emphasized repetition of words previously used by Christ. Asked by some concerning the resurrection He spoke of such as should be "accounted worthy to attain to that age and the resurrection out of [from among] the dead" - tees anastaseos tees ek nekron (Luke 20: 35). The expression "that age" must mean the millennial; for reaching the eternal ages is not a matter of our, but of our Saviour's, worthiness. And Scripture speaks of eternity as "ages" not as an "age." Moreover, "the coming age" (Mark 10: 30; Luke 18: 30) is the period when the Son of man shall sit on the "throne of His glory" and the apostles shall rule over Israel, i.e., the millennial age. See the parallel passage Matt. 19: 28. The translation "world" is a darkening of the divine counsel by a word that is inaccurate. The R.V. gives "age" in the margin. Darby translates by "the coming age" See pp. 96, 129."

GH Lang First Born Sons Their Rights and Risks; Chapter 8 The First Resurrection -A Prize, Paragraphs seven and eight[19]

The Scriptures gives us understanding of how mankind is affected by the three types of death: spiritual, physical, and eternal. The whole of the Bible records the effects of death from begging to end, with resurrection from the dead being Gods way to finalize the effects of death. Even when the Church persists in making disembodied men glorified upon death by going into

---

heaven, one thing is certain they still must be raised
from the dead. As mentioned before death is not
treated in Scripture as an answer instead it is viewed as
a great enemy. The last enemy to be overcome at the
Second Coming of Jesus Christ, is death itself.
Understanding the process by which God resolves
mankind's dilemma with this great enemy is of great
importance. Your very future and life depend on it.

Answering Some Objections
Question: Does not the Bible Teach the spirit of man, or
soul of man goes up to God upon death? Answer: As
previously noted up to the time of Jesus Christs death
the souls of men according to Scripture descended into
Hades. So, the only real question would be doing the
soul of man now ascend at death after Christ has been
raised from the dead?

"Who knoweth the spirit of man that goeth upward, and
the spirit of the beast that goeth downward to the
earth?" (Ecclesiastes 3:21) The answer is found in
Scriptures to the question posed by King Solomon.
Whose knows wither the spirit goes upward?

Some point out the Apostle Paul's experience. "I knew
such a man … how that he was caught up into paradise:"
(2 Corinthians 12:4) Seems to conclude the direction of
Paradise is now up and not down. However up closer
examination of the Greek in this passage, the word "up"
is not there in the original. The passage was originally

given by Paul with no indication of up or down, no direction at all. Just the fact he was caught away, not up. So, this passage is not conclusive evidence of Paradise now being removed from the underworld into heaven.

Another quote from Paul. '"To me to live is Christ, and to die is gain. ... For I am in a strait betwixt two, having the desire to depart and to be with Christ, for it is very far better:" (Philippians 1:21-23) "Whilst we are at home in the body, we are absent from the Lord. (For we walk by faith, not by sight.) We are confident I say, and willing rather to be absent from the body and present with the Lord:"
2 (Corinthians 5: 6-8.) It appears from these texts, that departed saints are with Christ, in a very especial sense. How can that be if they are not in heaven?'

Answer. Let us find the agreement. First death does not separate the child of Christ the born-again believer from Jesus Christ. Paradise is also called a "garden," so the place of the righteous departed is lovely, with the presence of the Lord. It acts as a place of consolation until the resurrection of the righteous. Now the debate. Paul's description could only mean heaven and not the underworld. This would be an inappropriate concept, as Paradise in the underworld is still a beautiful garden like environment with the Presence of God. Probably the prejudice comes from the reality of Hell with its severity and suffering? How can a place of beauty, Paradise, and a place of misery exist in close proximity in the underworld? Shouldn't a great distance separate the two? However, the record of Scriptures up to the time of the death and resurrection of Jesus Christ puts them in close proximity.

Luke 16:19-26[20]
19 There was a certain rich man, which was clothed in purple and fine linen, and fared sumptuously every day:
20 And there was a
certain beggar named Lazarus, which was
laid at his gate, full of sores,
21 And desiring to be fed with the
crumbs which fell from the rich
man's table: moreover dogs came and licked his sores.
22 And it came to pass, that the beggar died, and was carried by the angels into Abraham's bosom: the rich man also died, and was buried;
23 And in hell he lift up his eyes, being in torments, and seeth Abraham afar off, and Lazarus in his bosom.
24 And he cried and said, Father Abraham, have mercy on me, and send Lazarus, that dip the of his finger in water, and cool my tongue; for I am tormented in this flame.
25 But Abraham said, Son, remember that thou in thy lif etime receivedst thy good things, and likewise Lazarus evil things: but now he is comforted, and thou art tormented.
26 And beside all this, between us and you there is a

great gulf fixed: so that they which would pass
from to you cannot; neither can they
pass to us, that would come from thence.

Scriptures Point to No Man In Heaven

Another point neither of these passages actually
addresses the place of departed spirits. So once again
there is no Scripture which places the souls of
disembodied men in heaven. See this list of Scriptures
as evidence: (John 3: 13; Luke 20: 35; Heb. 11: 35b. cf.
Acts 2: 34; 7: 5; 2 Tim. 2: 18; Rev. 6: 9-11; 20: 4)

On the other hand, there is a great many passages
which do describe the place of the departed dead in the
underworld. Scriptures which testify the souls both of
the righteous and the wicked are in Hades. Including
Paradise which is below in the earth's interior as
indicated by many passages.

Another good question: How can the spirits of the
righteous be in Christ's presence, if they are in the
interior of the earth?'
Answer: The answer is simple, to be absent from the
body is to present with the Lord. The righteous dead in
Paradise before the coming of Jesus Christ were also in
God's presence, just not in Heaven. The prejudice being

is death keep us from Gods presence, but Paul says otherwise.

Now the big question: Has paradise been removed since the resurrection of Jesus Christ and altered since Christ rose and ascended?
Answer: The burden of proof still lies with the Scriptures. Are their passages which directly state Jesus Christ took Paradise from the underworld into Heaven? If so, what are they? Many say Ephesians 4:8-10 is that passage.
8 Wherefore he saith, when he ascended up on high, he led captivity captive, and gave gifts unto men.
9 (Now that he ascended, what is it but that he also descended first into the lower parts of the earth?
10 He that descended is the same also that ascended up far above all heavens, that he might fill all things.

However, my response is how can it be? As upon the resurrection of Jesus Christ the Church has been founded, and to help build upon the foundation God gave the Church gifts. This passage is about the Church, not the underworld, and gifts of men who are living given to the Church, not the dead.
What about the passage the Gates of Hell will not prevail against the Church? Isn't that proof when Jesus Christ ascended from the dead the Gates of Hell were opened wide, and the saints translated to heaven with Him?

Answer: The victory over Hades is not to be won till this corruptible has put on incorruption, and this mortal has put on immortality: (1 Corinthians 15:54-55) This Scripture speaks of a future day, our resurrection, and our becoming immortal. Instead, it proves the Gates of "Hades" still holds the dead both in Paradise and Hell until the resurrections are accomplished.

Paul clearly teaches when a man departs from his body upon death, he is being unclothed as a disembodied soul. As an unclothed soul makes the man not presentable before God. So, Paul emphasized, not that he wanted to be unclothed (death) but clothed upon with immortality. (Resurrection) Coming to understand death is part of the curse, a state in which man needs to be redeemed by resurrection. Souls are in Paradise awaiting their resurrection, the place of the disembodied unclothed dead in Christ. How much must the unclothing of the dead render them unfit for the In with Christ into the air. There the Lord waits, and they go downward to the earth to take up their bodies, then ascend and appear before Him to be judged. The assumption after having been already accepted by Him in heaven clothed with glory. However, this in no way is the record of Scriptures.

2 Corinthians 5:1-9[21]
1 For we
know that if our earthly house of this tabernacle were

---

[21]

dissolved, we have a building of God, an house not made with hands, eternal in the heavens.

2 For in this we groan, earnestly desiring to be clothed upon with our house which is from heaven:

3 If so be that being clothed we shall not be found naked.

4 For we that are in this tabernacle do groan, being burdened: not for that we would be unclothed, but clothed upon, that mortality might be swallowed up of life.

5 Now he that hath wrought us for the selfsame thing is God, who also hath given unto us earnest of.

6 Therefore we are always confident, knowing that, whilst we are at home in the body, absent from the Lord:

7 (For we walk by faith, not by sight:)

8 We are confident, I say, and willing rather to be absent from the body, and to be present with the Lord.

9 Wherefore we labour, that, whether present or absent, we may be accepted of him.

Now here are a list of some other Scriptures which demonstrate no man has yet ascended into Heaven, out from among the dead, except of course Jesus Christ. John 3:13[22]

22

13 And no man hath ascended up to heaven, but he that came down from heaven, even the Son of man which is in heaven.

Acts 2:34[23]
34 For David is not ascended into the heavens: but he saith himself, The Lord said unto my Lord, Sit thou on my right hand. Clearly from this passage, King David a man after Gods own heart has not yet ascended fifty days after the resurrection of Jesus Christ. So, if Paradise was removed into Heaven when Jesus Christ was raised from the dead, why was King David not raised?

Revelation 6:9-11[24]
9 And when he had opened the fifth seal, I saw under the altar the souls of them that were slain for the word of God, and for the testimony which they held:
10 And they cried with a loud voice, saying, how long, O Lord, holy and true, dost thou not judge and avenge our blood on them that dwell on the earth?
11 And white robes were given unto every one of them; and it was said unto them, that they should rest yet for a little season, until their fellow servants also and their brethren, that should be killed as they were, should be fulfilled.

23
24

How is it the souls of the righteous dead are under the alter in a disembodied state even far into the final judgments of God? If glorification upon death were the Christians true state, should not those who were martyred for Christian attain to some of the highest glory? Yet these were still crying out for justice, and wanting to be brought up from under the alter? If we conclude the alter to be the brazen alter on earth, these are the departed souls of righteous martyrs still in Paradise in the underworld.

Chapter 4
The Effects of a Sin Nature

The Bible gives us the complete record of deaths origin, and its ending. In the beginning of God's creation of the heaven and earth there was no death, no decay, no corruption. Into a world without sin God created His man, after His image, and gave him dominion over all the earth. In this world free from sin, moral decay, free of corruption and death, Adam was given charge. However, this all changed when Adam agreed to disobey God, and sin entered the world, and death by sin.
The Scriptures record the incredible transformation which took place with the "fall of man." The heights from which mankind fell, and the depth of depravity which resulted cannot really be comprehended, as we have a hard time understanding what Adam forfeited.

However, the effects of sin and death are daily realities which rule over fallen creation.

Life and death are now interrelated, however in the beginning it was not so. In this present age death became man's natural enemy. In death the soul of man separates out of his body into an unnatural state. So unnatural is a disembodied soul, God must provide the way back to unite soul and body to save the man's life. In the process of saving a man from the fall salvation is not complete until the soul of man in the state of death is completely reversed and reunited to his original body. The whole of the Christian salvation is based upon the resurrection. Gods ability to raise the souls of the departed back into their original bodies and make both body and soul immortal and glorified is promised.

Death came into the world by sin. It is just that simple and complex. The first act of sin committed by Adam is called original sin. As the result of original sin, the nature of sin manifested in the fallen man as spiritual death. The day which Adam and Eve ate in disobedience to God, they died spiritually on the inside. The human spirit died to its life and connection to God, and Adam was instantly alienated from God, and under His judgment and wrath. God and man now longer had sweet communion instead man ran from God and hid his sin under a fig leaves covering. Of course, the fig leaves did not cover the sin in Gods eyes only deluded man into thinking it was hidden. Sin and death had taken hold of original man changed his nature, making man a child of wrath by nature.

So complete is the nature of sin and death inside fallen man it is passed on to his prosperity. The nature of fallen man is called the Adamic nature and was not what God had originally intended or designed. The nature of sin's corruption is to the utmost, making man totally deprived, and incapable of escaping sin and deaths dominion. The facts of sin and death speak for themselves as everyman who has ever been born into this present fallen evil age has received the Adamic nature. For all who derive their life from Adam are by nature depraved by a life of sin, and the soul which sins shall die. By Adamic original sin death entered the world, and sin and death have passed upon all mankind by nature.

Romans 5:12-14[25]
12 Wherefore, as by one-man sin entered into the world, and death by sin; and so, death passed upon all men, for that all have sinned:
13 (For until the law sin was in the world: but sin is not imputed when there is no law.
14 Nevertheless death reigned from Adam to Moses, even over them that had not sinned after the similitude of Adam's transgression, who is the figure of him that was to come.

25

What man is by nature, is now the result of sin and death. Spiritual death has resulted in a nature which makes man a natural born enemy to God. The Bible describes this condition as a child of wrath, under the judgment and wrath of God. So, serve is this condition God cursed it putting the sentence of eternal judgment upon sin. God has pronounced judgment upon all fallen humanity. Charged guilty of sin alienated from the life of God because of spiritual death and blinded by a calloused heart of sin.

Ephesians 4:17-19[26]
17 This I say therefore, and testify in the Lord, that ye henceforth walk not as other Gentiles walk, in the vanity of their mind,
18 Having the understanding darkened, being alienated from the life of God through the ignorance that is in them, because of the blindness of their heart:
19 Who being past feeling have given themselves over unto lasciviousness, to work all uncleanness with greediness.

Ephesians 2:1-3[27]
1 And you hath he quickened, who were dead in trespasses and sins.
2 Wherein in time past ye walked according to the course of this world, according to the prince of the

---

[26]
[27]

power of the air, the spirit that now worketh in the children of disobedience:
3 Among whom also we all had our conversation in times past in the lusts of our flesh, fulfilling the desires of the flesh and of the mind; and were by nature the children of wrath, even as others.

Adamic nature is given to every man by birth are hostile to God by nature and break His laws. For every act of sin is a transgression of the law of God. Natural man is born into this world with an Adamic sin nature, and as every soul which sins shall die. For this reason, death has reigned in the life of every single man. So natural is sin and death to modern man we have incorporated its effect into all our lives. It is natural for a man to curse, sin, and hate God. In the process of being convicted of our sin, we like Adam hide behind our fig leaves in denial of our sins.

Forces Which Control Life

With all the division going on among the nations, terrorism, anger, and hate, even bloodshed, we sometimes forget we are dealing with forces which we cannot control. So destructive, so vital to our life are these forces the Bible labels them the law of sin and death. Is it any wonder when men have prided themselves in human achievement, and yet at the same time the darkness of human nature still comes to light? It is strange to live in a world where technology has become so advanced yet will still use it to kill and hate one another.

Recently, I have taken note about the enormous amount of death which has come about by natural events. Like earthquakes, floods, hurricanes, volcanos, labeled as acts from Mother Nature. It is like the world is convulsing and letting out all this death and dying. The things I have mentioned, are out of the control of man's ability as the result are subjected to forces greater than us. Yet mankind still persists; we can fix the world and bring world peace and unity. Even the Church has gotten caught up into thinking its job is to make for a worldwide Christian culture. Only our own delusion and denial would lead us to believe we can control forces which are far greater than our capability.

What is the problem? Sin and death are constant, these laws determine the course of every man, as no man has ever escaped their power to control life and death. Leading men to despair not knowing how to overcome the power of sin in their own lives. Have you have ever attempted to "fix your life," make yourself better? You will see the nature of your flesh rise up, and the laws of sin and death will make you realize without Christ you are powerless over the laws of sin and death. The only way to escape is from the free gift of eternal life. In Jesus Christ must man be born again.

However, even the Church has lost sight of the depravity of sin being tempted to speak on the greatness of human potential. Maybe you are a Christian who is in distress, and you are in a great battle with sin and darkness. You can see the world getting darker all the while men are in deeper denial acting like they can live in control of their life. While you see the growing issue of a lawless world spinning out of control, being pulled along by forces of sin and death.

Why are people increasingly unhappy, empty dissatisfied feeling they are just going through the motions? At the end of the age, the Bible speaks of perilous times where sin and death are going to come to a head. In the midst of all man's pride, all the technological advancement you can feel dark forces which are out of our control. The darkness is growing, the world is shaking, and culture is unraveling. You cannot fix it as the nations are moving towards deep darkness where men will revel in darkness, and lawlessness will abound. Can you see it, can you feel it? The world is rapidly changing moving into an antichrist mentality, and soon the world will be heaving in the Great Tribulation.

How can you escape? It is time to recognize the law of sin and death are out of your control. As a Christian you have been born again, and you must live by the law of the Spirit of Life in Christ. The only way out is keeping your entire life all about Jesus Christ. Wherever you refuse to give up the self-life you will find yourself being draw along further away from living for Jesus Christ.

Yes, many Christians will justify their sins, and fleshly deeds, but they walk in darkness. The way out is to deny yourself pick up the Cross and fellowship in the sufferings of Christ. You must recognize this world is not your home, and you are on a pilgrimage towards the Second Coming of the Lord. Along the way your life in Christ becomes springs of life and pools of refreshing in a dying world.

If you can see all this then you are awake, and God has given your eyes to see and an understanding heart. Do not be surprised if more and more Christians seem like they are asleep in the light. As in the times of advancing darkness the Church is moving Christians away from Christ, and more into apostasy. More than I have ever seen Christians have compromised their faith and are walking in deception.

Running from God

In the Adamic life it is natural to run and hide from God. The guilt and condemnation of sin just like Adam experienced makes us to want to cover up and deny our transgressions. However, the law of sin and death is not a respecter of persons, so what we sow we shall reap. The consequences of what we do with Gods laws really does play into our life's experience. The consequences can be observed both now, and eternally. For whosoever sins transgresses the law, for sin is the breaking of Gods law.

1 John 3:4[28]
4 Whosoever committeth sin transgresseth also the law:
for sin is the transgression of the law.

So, running and hiding from God because of our sins is
the normal course of life since the fall of man into
original sin. In this way, in most cases we simply are our
own worst enemy. We are driven by our sinful desires
to our own demise. We can suffer great harm in our
bodies or in our minds on a personal level as well as
effecting those around our lives. Sin can never bring life
even though we are tempted with is seductive power.
The lust of the eyes, the lust of the flesh and mind,
coupled with the pride of life has convinced man he has
no need for God. No need for man to obey His laws.
What is the outcome and consequences? By their lustful
desires driven by their sin nature fallen man has sown
to their own destruction, or others.

Resulting in sickness or diseases, premature deaths, and
great suffering. How readily do men suffer from the
results of sinful practices in their bodies and minds. The
Scriptures even warn Christians about their sinful
behaviors. As the result of unconfessed sins, and selfish
sinful practices, or in the treatment of other persons the
Scriptures warn of Christians reaping sickness and even
premature death.

28

1 Corinthians 11:27-32[29]

27 Wherefore whosoever shall eat this bread, and drink this cup of the Lord, unworthily, shall be guilty of the body and blood of the Lord.

28 But let a man examine himself, and so let him eat of that bread, and drink of that cup.

29 For he that eateth and drinketh unworthily, eateth and drinketh damnation to himself, not discerning the Lord's body.

30 For this cause many are weak and sickly among you, and many sleep.

31 For if we would judge ourselves, we should not be judged.

32 But when we are judged, we are chastened of the Lord, that we should not be condemned with the world.

Gods Judgment of Sin

When Adam committed the original sin what kind of effect did mankind experience as the result of the fall? All humanity was cursed under sin and death, alienated from God, and under His wrath? The effect of sin and death is so catastrophic, natural fallen man is born a rebel a natural enemy to God a child of Satan, and a child of wrath. Now there is no escape from the curse of the effects of original sin as natural fallen man hates God a consequence of a corrupted sin nature. Fallen man with a sin nature has lost his ability to conform to

---

29

likeness and image of God. The fall of mankind into original sin is so complete, Satan becomes the lord over fallen cursed humanity, and fallen men are children of the devil. Born alienated from God from the womb natural man loves the darkness and hates the light and will not come to the light to have the evil deeds exposed.

Most men live in the darkness their whole lives under the wrath of God having their minds darkened alienated from the life of God, because of the ignorance which is in them. Now natural fallen man may differ in their levels of actual practices of sins, some being more exceeding wicked then the rest. However, God still concludes all under sin, with the death penalty given to all. So, when natural fallen man born alienated from God, a natural enemy, a child of wrath, dies in their sins God sends them to Hell to await eternal judgment. After, casts unredeemed man in the Lake of Fire to be eternally punished in the fire which is never extinguished. So, the wicked go astray from the womb, are totally alienated from God are cursed under sin and death will die in their sins awakening in the fires of Hell.

Ephesians 2:1-3[30]
1 And you hath he quickened, who were dead in trespasses and sins.
2 Wherein in time past ye walked according to the course of this world, according to the prince of the

---

30

power of the air, the spirit that now worketh in the children of disobedience:

3 Among whom also we all had our conversation in times past in the lusts of our flesh, fulfilling the desires of the flesh and of the mind; and were by nature the children of wrath, even as others.

Now will God have mercy in the deaths of fallen man who lived there under His wrath. On the contrary, when man born in original sin dies alienated from God no hope of grace or mercy remains. For it is appointed once for a man to die then comes God's judgment. (Hebrews 9:27) Upon death having refused the calling of God their entire lives, no hope of mercy remains. Hell is their reality judged by God without God's remorse, and without mercy, or any reduction in the length of the sentence or the severity of punishment.

What is ironic all of heaven rejoices and praises God when the final judgments are seen in the earth, as God pours out the vials of wrath at the Second Coming of Jesus Christ.
(Revelation 19:1-5)

Will God tolerate sin? Will God cover up the sins of fallen man? Then why would God have the punishment of Hell? Or put man in eternal judgment, with no hope of escape or relief for an eternity? No even the best of men who lived lives of luxury while alive, and who were highly praised by men when they die in their sins will escape the endless suffering of the Lake of Fire. Now will the modern Church preach the false doctrine there is "no Hell?" Will the modern Church delude men with "seeker sensitivity," so as not to offend fallen man? So as not to waken and warn them to the dangers of God's judgment? His wrath without mercy, and their portion in the Lake of Fire?

How far has the Church fallen when Christians can sin carelessly, and when the saints live ungodly immoral lives? The Scriptures warn "do not be partakers" with the adulterer, with the sexually immoral, with those who love this present world who provoke the Lord to jealousy. Christians do you do not know for the sake of these things the wrath of God comes to judge the "sons of disobedience," therefore do not be partakers with them. Will a God who has no mercy upon a man who dies in his sin, whose soul is sent to Hell then overlook the same sinful behaviors in Christians? Be sure God is an impartial judge and will judge every man according to their works.

Ephesians 5:1-7[31]
1 Be ye therefore followers of God, as dear children.
2 And walk-in love, as Christ also hath loved us, and hath given himself for us an offering and a sacrifice to God for a sweet smelling savour.

31

3 But fornication, and all uncleanness, or covetousness, let it not be once named among you, as becometh saints.

4 Neither filthiness, nor foolish talking, nor jesting, which are not convenient: but rather giving of thanks.

5 For this ye know, that no whoremonger, nor unclean person, nor covetous man, who is an idolater, hath any inheritance in the kingdom of Christ and of God.

6 Let no man deceive you with vain words: for because of these things cometh the wrath of God upon the children of disobedience.

7 Be not ye therefore partakers with them.

Section II
What Is Hell

Chapter 5
The Reality of Hell

Gods judgment on sin and death comes from the fall of man. In order to gain proper understanding of eternal judgment, we must ask the question; "what is Hell?" Today many Christian teachers are attempting to distance themselves from the offense of Hell, and souls which are suffering in Hell Fire. In order to discredit the doctrine of Hell many attempt to say Hell is just an allegory, a symbol, not real fact, or a real place.

However, both the Old Testament and New Testament identify the place of the unrighteous departed. The disembodied soul of the wicked presides in Hell upon death. While their bodies are placed in the grave returning to the dust from which they are made, the soul of the wicked must suffer the Judgment of God in Hell Fire.

Hell, then is a real location a part of the underworld, one of the several parts of the underworld. Part of what is called Hades. As formerly expressed, Hades has at least three distinct locations, Hell, Paradise, and Tartarus. The Book of Revelation also describes a place which houses end time evil spirits called the Abyss which is also from the underworld. The Abyss is also the place where Satan is chained by God during the 1000-year rule of Jesus Christ on earth, the Millennial Kingdom age.

Many philosophers have theorized on Hell giving their versions of Hell's torment and suffering. One very popular version of Hell came from Dante, a poet philosopher from 1300's, wrote of eternal punishment in a production also called, The Divine Comedy

"The Divine Comedy (Italian: Divina Commedia [diˈviːna komˈmɛːdja]) is a long narrative poem by Dante Alighieri, begun c. 1308 and completed in 1320, a year before his death in 1321. It is widely considered to be the preeminent work in Italian literature[1] and one of the greatest works of world literature.[2] The poem's imaginative vision of the afterlife is representative of

the medieval worldview as it had developed in the Western Church by the 14th century. It helped establish the Tuscan language, in which it is written, as the standardized Italian language.[3] It is divided into three parts: Inferno, Purgatorio, and Paradiso.
The narrative describes Dante's travels through Hell, Purgatory, and Paradise or Heaven,[4] while allegorically the poem represents the soul's journey towards God.[5] Dante draws on medieval Christian theology and philosophy, especially Thomistic philosophy and the Summa Theologica of Thomas Aquinas.[6] Consequently, the Divine Comedy has been called "the Summa in verse".[7] In Dante's work, Virgil is presented as human reason and Beatrice is presented as divine knowledge.[8]" (Wikipedia)[32]

However, Dante drew from Mid evil philosophical beliefs and was heavily influenced by the philosopher Aristotle, and Catholicism. In Dante's Hell, the formation of Hell was the result of the fall of Satan before the creation of the world and has Satan and evil spirits in its control. In Dante's Hell certain sins require a greater depth into Hell with greater punishment, also contains a Catholic version of purgatory. All these are just philosophical versions of Hell which deviate from the Biblical facts of Hell.

Fact one; God created Hell for the Devil and his angels. The creation of Hell is by God, and God is the source of punishment, and the one in control of Hell. God is the creator of all regions of heaven and earth as the underworld is also a portion of God's creation of the earth. The time of Hells creation may or may not be before the fall of Satan, and the rebellion of one third of Gods angels with Satan. As God has omniscience, He was not taken by surprise regarding Satan's rebellion and fall from His original order of creation. God expelled Satan who at the time of his rebellion was called the angel Lucifer. After the expulsion of Satan, God then creates man after His image and gives him authority over all things related to the care of the earth. Gods delegated authority to Adam also included Satan and his evil spirits in relationship to the care and rule over the earth.

We do not know the time frame between Satan's exclusion from heaven, and the creation of man. Neither do we know if Hell was already in existence by the time of man's creation. However, we know the original order of creation before the fall of man into Satan's temptation, and man at that time had the dominion over the earth, not Satan.

The dominion over the earth was delegated by God, as the truest since of rule is by God Himself. As the earth is the Lords and the fulness thereof. With the fall of Adam into original sin a major shift in authority and governance resulted. Satan became the over lord of the world, over fallen man as the Prince of the Power of the

Air. Even when Satan tempted Jesus Christ in the wilderness Satan said the glory of the world's kingdoms were given to him. The worlds kingdoms are ruled by the rule of the kingdom of darkness. Ruled by the dark Prince Satan, and a kingdom of dark evil spirits makes the kingdoms of this world are under Satan's authority. Adam is the one which gave his God given authority away to Satan at the fall of man. All these beliefs have been discussed and theorized but one fact remains, Satan has a Kingdom of darkness on this earth, and rules over fallen humanity.

Matthew 25:41-46[33]
41 Then shall he say also unto them on the left hand, depart from me, ye cursed, into everlasting fire, prepared for the devil and his angels:
42 For I was an hungred, and ye gave me no meat: I was thirsty, and ye gave me no drink:
43 I was a stranger, and ye took me not in: naked, and ye clothed me not: sick, and in prison, and ye visited me not.
44 Then shall they also answer him, saying, Lord, when saw we thee an hungred, or athirst, or a stranger, or naked, or sick, or in prison, and did not minister unto thee?
45 Then shall he answer them, saying, Verily I say unto you, inasmuch as ye did it not to one of the least of these, ye did it not to me.

33

46 And these shall go away into everlasting punishment: but the righteous into life eternal.

Fact Two: Satan Is Not in Hell. Many people by old fashioned myths believe the dwelling place of the Devil and evil spirits is in Hell. However, Satan in not in Hell instead he is the Prince of the Power of the Air. His influence and kingdom are upon the earth. Satan as a fallen angel is able to inhabit not only the earth also the heaven immediately above the earth. It is clear from Scriptures Satan is not put into the Abyss, or into the underworld until after the Battle of Armageddon at the Second Coming of Jesus Christ, and the start of the Millennial age.

Revelation 20:1-3[34]
1 And I saw an angel come down from heaven, having the key of the bottomless pit and a great chain in his hand.
2 And he laid hold on the dragon, that old serpent, which is the Devil, and Satan, and bound him a thousand years,
3 And cast him into the bottomless pit, and shut him up, and set a seal upon him, that he should deceive the nations no more, till the thousand years should be fulfilled: and after that he must be loosed a little season.

34

Until the time of being chained into the abyss Satan is able by right to operate from the immediate heaven and earth over fallen man. Satan is not in Hell right now, or his evil spirits instead they deceive and torment mankind on this side of the grave on earth.

Who then is in charge of Hell if Satan is not? The answer is simple God made Hell, Hell Fire, Eternal Fire, for Satan and his evil spirits. However, all these are also now used to punish the wicked after the fall of man. The only beings which are suffering in Hell at this time are the souls of unredeemed humanity. The torment of Hell is not from the presence of Satan as his kingdom rule does not include Hell, or any portion of the underworld.

Matthew 25:41[35]
41 Then shall he say also unto them on the left hand, depart from me, ye cursed, into everlasting fire, prepared for the devil and his angels.

Fact Three: God is in control of Hell. This might be surprising to many Christians, God not only created Hell, He also is the one who presides over it. Yes, Hell was originally made for the Devil and evil spirits in their fall and rebellion to Gods authority. However, no evil spirit has been sent into Hell at this time. So, the inhabitants of Hell are only the disembodied souls of men, women, and children who have died outside of salvation in Jesus Christ. The torment of Hell is real, as well as the

---

35

suffering souls the punishment which comes from Hell's fire not evil spirits. The source of suffering is not the torment of Satan punishing disembodied souls as the result of sinful lives. Satan is not in control of punishment in Hell, neither is Satan the judge of fallen man. Instead, God is the judge over all humanity, and rewards the righteous dead with salvation in Paradise, and the unrighteous dead with punishment in Hell.

Fact Four: The wicked departed suffer in Hell's Fire. The source of suffering is a fire which torments the souls of the unrighteous dead. The fire comes from God who has judged and condemned the souls of the unrighteous dead to Hell Fire. God places the unrighteous dead into the Fire of Hell as part of the judicial process of eternal judgment. The damned souls will suffer in the flames of Hell as punishment until the time of the second resurrection. At that time, the unrighteous will be raised up out of Hell to stand before God at the Great White Throne Judgment. Some men will have existed in Hell for several thousands of years since the time of their death before standing at the Great White Throne Judgment.

The fact the wicked departed suffer in Hell fire is a fact of Scripture. Here is a sample teaching from Jesus Christ which demonstrates the suffering of the wicked departed in Hells Fire.

Luke 16:19-31[36]

19 There was a certain rich man, which was clothed in purple and fine linen, and fared sumptuously every day:

20 And there was a certain beggar named Lazarus, which was laid at his gate, full of sores,

21 And desiring to be fed with the crumbs which fell from the rich man's table: moreover, the dogs came and licked his sores.

22 And it came to pass, that the beggar died, and was carried by the angels into Abraham's bosom: the rich man also died, and was buried.

23 And in hell he lift up his eyes, being in torments, and seeth Abraham afar off, and Lazarus in his bosom.

24 And he cried and said, Father Abraham, have mercy on me, and send Lazarus, that he may dip the tip of his finger in water, and cool my tongue; for I am tormented in this flame.

25 But Abraham said, Son, remember that thou in thy lifetime receivedst thy good things, and likewise Lazarus evil things: but now he is comforted, and thou art tormented.

26 And beside all this, between us and you there is a great gulf fixed: so that they which would pass from hence to you cannot; neither can they pass to us, that would come from thence.

27 Then he said, I pray thee therefore, father, that thou wouldest send him to my father's house:

28 For I have five brethren; that he may testify unto them, lest they also come into this place of torment.

36

29 Abraham saith unto him, They have Moses and the prophets; let them hear them.
30 And he said, Nay, father Abraham: but if one went unto them from the dead, they will repent.
31 And he said unto him, If they hear not Moses and the prophets, neither will they be persuaded, though one rose from the dead.

Was the rich man a person which thought after I die, I will be in Hell? Of course, not the rich man was what everyone else wanted to be like. A person with the worlds goods is often thought to be blessed by God. However, this particular rich man despised his neighbor, the beggar Lazarus who daily begged at the rich man's gate hoping just to get some crumbs of food. The rich man had no sense to be his brother's keeper, and did not use his wealth to honor God, and gave nothing to Lazarus the poor beggar. Is this not the same behaviors which are exhibited by many wealthy people of the world today? Does the world then deem them worthy of Hell upon their deaths? Jesus Christ taught Godless living will not be overlooked, even though the world might even praise a man of great wealth.

Notice when these men both died their souls did not go into heaven, instead both men were taken in the underworld. The beggar Lazarus was taken by angels into the underworld in his disembodied soul into Paradise where he joined Abraham who was awaiting the resurrection. While the rich man upon awakening from his separation of soul and body lifted up his eyes from Hell. God obviously knew the rich man as a wicked unrighteous man while alive on earth. Now judged to Hell by God, the rich man's soul was in torment in the flames of Hell fire. Notice there was no mention of Satan, or evil spirits just the torment which came upon the rich man's soul from Hells fire. Did the rich man choose the underworld and Hell fire? Of course, not no man in the right mind believes they are deserving of the judicial fire of Gods judgment in Hell. Upon this blindness millions of men, women and children die every year and are found in the fires of Gods judgment, Hell Fire.

Notice how the souls of both the rich man and beggar in the underworld could think, feel, reason, communicate and recognize each other. Life after death proves not to be the end of existence instead an intermediate state before the soul is reunited with the body for final judgment. From Hell the rich man communicated with Abraham across a great gulf which divided Hell from Paradise. He cried out for Abraham to have mercy and send the beggar Lazarus to dip the tip of his finger in water just to give him a little relief from the tormenting flame. Also notice how Abraham and Lazarus were not in torment even though they both were in the state of death as disembodied souls. The point was Paradise provided relief for Abraham and the righteous beggar, while Hell a place of torment for the souls of the unrighteous. Both places were really experienced in the persons who were confined there. Real life experiences of death and life in death the rich man in Hells suffering, Lazarus in Paradise with Gods comfort.

Did the rich man think his brothers would escape Hell after seeing Hells judgment? After the truth of Hell fire broke into the reality of the rich mans after life. He feared members of his family who also lived Godless lives would be sent to Hell too. What a difference in life after death perspectives. From godless men who deny the reality of Hell as compared to those who are in Hell and are tormented by its flames. The rich man begged Abraham to send someone to his father's house to warn his father and five brothers not to come to Hell. However, Abraham said the have the voice of the prophets written in the Word of God which warned mankind to escape the coming wrath of God. If they would not believe the Word of God Gods prophets neither would they believe the one who would warn them after raising up from among the dead, Jesus Christ. Sadly, even though Jesus Christ has come back from among the dead men still mock Hell and refuse His testimony. Fallen man is blind to his eternal fate when he mocks the resurrection, and their future existence in Hell.

Fact Four:
Upon Death the Soul of the Damned Have No Escape

Hell is just part of eternal judgment. Once a man dies then comes the judgment. For those who are eternally judged to Hell there will be no future mercy, or way of escape. Some Christians would like to think Hell is an act of Gods mercy, or a display of His unfailing love.

However, I want to assure you Hell has nothing to do with love and mercy instead it is all about the wrath of God, and His judgment. Unlike the Catholic Purgatory which offers a man a second chance after death to atone for this life of sin, Hell has not second chance, no mercy, and no way of escape.

Many modern-day Christians might be offended at the thought after a man dies, he suffers in Hell fire. If his life was not redeemed by the Cross, God's judgment places the soul of the unredeemed into Hell to pay the debut of sin. To refuse Gods way of escape through the Cross, only brings eternal judgment, not salvation. No mercy or forgiveness, and no escape from the eternal punishment.
Hell is not forever, as after the Second Resurrection men in Hell are raised back into their bodies to face judgement at the Great White Throne. Whosoever's name is not found written in the Book of Life is then cast from Hell into the Lake of Fire. In this case Hell comes to an end, but the fire of eternal suffering never stops burning and tormenting the men who were in Hell. Who are now placed after the Great White Throne into the everlasting fire, the Lake of Fire? The judgment

is eternal and so is the suffering only this time the body of the man is also included in eternal suffering in the Lake of Fire. There is no end, no way of escape, and no mercy for any man who refuses Jesus Christ. Only eternal judgment in Gods judicial fire.

Revelation 14:9-11[37]
9 And the third angel followed them, saying with a loud voice, if any man worship the beast and his image, and receive his mark in his forehead, or in his hand,
10 The same shall drink of the wine of the wrath of God, which is poured out without mixture into the cup of his indignation; and he shall be tormented with fire and brimstone in the presence of the holy angels, and in the presence of the Lamb:
11 And the smoke of their torment ascendeth up for ever and ever: and they have no rest day nor night, who worship the beast and his image, and whosoever receiveth the mark of his name.

What is the worm that will not die in Hell?
Mark 9:41-48[38]
41 For whosoever shall give you a cup of water to drink in my name, because ye belong to Christ, verily I say unto you, he shall not lose his reward.
42 And whosoever shall offend one of these little ones that believe in me, it is better for him that a millstone

---

[37]
[38]

were hanged about his neck, and he were cast into the sea.

43 And if thy hand offend thee, cut it off: it is better for thee to enter into life maimed, than having two hands to go into hell, into the fire that never shall be quenched:

44 Where their worm dieth not, and the fire is not quenched.

45 And if thy foot offend thee, cut it off: it is better for thee to enter halt into life, than having two feet to be cast into hell, into the fire that never shall be quenched:

46 Where their worm dieth not, and the fire is not quenched.

47 And if thine eye offend thee, pluck it out: it is better for thee to enter into the kingdom of God with one eye, than having two eyes to be cast into hell fire:

48 Where their worm dieth not, and the fire is not quenched.

In Mark 9, when Jesus says, Where their worm does not die and the fire is not quenched, He is quoting from Isaiah 66:24: "They will go out and look on the dead bodies of those who rebelled against me; the worms that eat them will not die, the fire that burns them will not be quenched, and they will be loathsome to all mankind." In both texts the word translated as worm, means worm, just like the fire means fire. In Gehenna fire, the Lake of Fire is where this passage speaks. Both the fire and the worms feed upon the unrighteous dead for all eternity. Their condition in the Lake of Fire is an abhorring, an object of loathsome horror. If any man were to know in reality the Lake of Fire as his final state for all eternity, no man in his right mind would ever want to be there.

Isaiah 66:22-24[39]
22 For as the new heavens and the new earth, which I will make, shall remain before me, saith the Lord, so shall your seed and your name remain.
23 And it shall come to pass, that from one new moon to another, and from one sabbath to another, shall all flesh come to worship before me, saith the Lord.
24 And they shall go forth, and look upon the carcases of the men that have transgressed against me: for their worm shall not die, neither shall their fire be quenched; and they shall be an abhorring unto all flesh,

Taken at face value, this text is one of the most horrific descriptions of what hell fire is like. The thought of eternal torment likened to maggots eating away at a rotting corpse is one of the most gross images of Hell Christ revealed. Hell is so awful that Christ said, figuratively speaking, it is better to cut off the hand that causes you to sin than to end up in hell (Mark 9:43).

Some Bible teachers do not believe the worms to be literal. Instead, the worms are a figure of speech instead the worm refers to a man's conscience. Those in hell being completely cut off from God exist with an unceasing tormenting guilty conscience. The guilt and torment are like a worm which gnaws away at its victim with a remorse that can never be resolved. No matter what the word worm refers to, the most important thing to be gained from these words of Christ is that we should do everything in our power to escape the horrors of hell.

Is Annihilationism Biblical

Annihilationism is the belief that unbelievers will not experience an eternity of suffering in hell but will instead be extinguished after death.

"Annihilationism (also known as extinctionism or destructionism[1]) is a belief that after the final judgment some human beings and all fallen angels (all of the damned) will be totally destroyed so as to not exist, or that their consciousness will be extinguished,[2] rather than suffer everlasting torment in hell (often synonymized with the lake of fire).
Annihilationism is directly related to the doctrine of conditional immortality, the idea that a human soul is not immortal unless it is given eternal life.
Annihilationism asserts that God will eventually destroy the wicked, leaving only the righteous to live on in immortality. Some annihilationist's (e.g., Seventh-day Adventists) believe God's love is scripturally described

as an all-consuming fire[3] and that sinful creatures cannot exist in God's presence. Thus, those who elect to reject salvation through their free will are eternally destroyed because of the inherent incompatibility of sin with God's holy character. Seventh-day Adventists posit that living in eternal hell is a false doctrine of pagan origin, as the Wicked will perish (as the Bible says) in the Lake of fire.[4][5][6][7] Jehovah's Witnesses believe that there can be no punishment after death because the dead cease to exist.[8]
Annihilationism stands in contrast to both the traditional and long-standing belief in eternal torture in the lake of fire, and the belief that everyone will be saved (universal reconciliation or simply "universalism")." (Wikipedia)[40]

Annihilationism is the invention of man who twists Scriptures in dealing with the offense of Hell, and the Lake of Fire. Its attraction has to do with a loving God who would punish men outside of His salvation for an eternity in torment in the Lake of Fire. Those who argue for Annihilationism must do so by downplaying the Biblical doctrines of Gods judgment on sin, the justice of God, and eternal judgment.

The eternity of the soul must be denied by Annihilates, as the Scriptures prove once a man comes into existence his soul remains eternal. So even in Hell the soul of man functions with thought, communication,

40

feeling, and emotion. Death does not cause the soul of man to cease to exist, or even to enter into soul sleep. Instead, the disembodied soul of the unsaved exists fully aware in Hells fire and is in the torment of Gods judicial fire. At the second resurrection of the souls of the unredeemed are taken from Hell and reunited with their bodies to be cast soul and body into the Lake of Fire. For all eternity, the unredeemed resurrected man is taken from Hell and placed into the Lake of Fire who will suffer torment day and night. This is in fact the reality of the eternity of the human soul. Those who are redeemed live forever in the New Heavens and New Earth, as well those who are eternally damned in the Lake of Fire. As the Scriptures prove the soul of man once created is an eternal soul.

Also, Annihilationism attempts to argue the detention of eternity, Instead of everlasting, Annihilationism attempts to put the word, "age ending," in place of eternity. The Greek word: aionion, is the basis of argument which sometimes can be rightly translated age ending. In specific cases refers to a measured amount of time. However, in the New Testament aionion can also mean an eternity, especially related to some passages which teach an eternal length of time. A prime example of interpretation of eternity as compared to age ending would be Matthew 25:46 where Gods final judgements are represented as eternal.

"Then they (the goats)will go away to eternal punishment, but the righteous (sheep) to eternal life." In this verse, the same Greek word is used to refer to the destiny of the wicked and the righteous. If the wicked are only tormented for an age ending time, then the righteous will only experience life in the New Heavens and New Earth for a limited time. Instead, believers will be in New heavens and New Earth forever, and unbelievers will be in Hell Fire forever. (Lake of Fire)

Another object of annihilationist's is the length of time of eternal punishment in the Lake of Fire. They reason away the Word of God attempting to philosophize it would be unjust for God to punish a man for all eternity for just short lifetime of sin in comparison. Once again, the reasoning of human wisdom fails to adequate reveal the eternal consequences of sin. It is not a matter of the length of time which we sin instead the judgment upon sin. Death, corruption, and Hell are the consequences of sin which cannot be overruled by human efforts. Only the Cross of Jesus Christ is able to pay the debut to the curse of Sin and Death. Man is hopelessly lost without escape from the Law of Sin and Death. Its power is to rule over fallen humanity, just like any another law has been proven throughout human history. The wages of sin are death, and for the unredeemed is finally resolved in the Second death, the Lake Fire for all eternity. Salvation is eternal, so is Hell Fire.

Now human sympathy also plays a role in Annihilationism. For those in the New Heavens and New Earth could never be satisfied or fulfilled knowing some of their friends or relatives are burning in the Lake of Fire. However, the Scriptures reveal just the opposite when the righteous judgment of God are viewed in the earth after the Second Coming, the sense of injustice, or inequity will pass away. There will be no more death in the New Heavens and New Earth neither suffering nor pain for the redeemed. Instead of suffering the loss of our loved ones the way we do now, with our eyes wide open will be in complete agreement with God knowing they do not belong in the New Heavens and New Earth. We will come to see how Gods judgments complete His love, mercy, and justice and is completely equitable. Our loved ones are condemned by their own actions, and refusal of Jesus Christ are justly punished.

Keeping these facts in mind, Hell and the Lake of Fire must be one of the primary reasons Jesus Christ went to the Cross as our sin substitute. Knowing the human soul is not extinguished after death but suffers an eternity in Hell fire if no redemption from sin and death. Modern Christianity has lost sight of eternity, and eternal consequences. Sad to say, many Christians no longer believe in the judgment of Hell, and therefore no longer warn their friends and relatives to flee from the wrath to come.

Hell is perhaps a primary reason why God sent Jesus Christ to pay the penalty for our sins. Being "extinguished" after death is no fate to dread, but an eternity in hell most definitely is. Jesus' death was an infinite death, paying our infinite sin debt so that we would not have to pay it in hell for eternity.
(2 Corinthians 5:21). When we place our faith in Him, we are saved, forgiven, cleansed, and promised an eternal home in the New Heavens and Earth. But if we reject God's gift of eternal life, we will face the eternal consequences of that decision.

Will Satan Be Saved

"In early Christian theological usage apocatastasis meant the ultimate restoration of all things to their original state, which early exponents believed would still entail a purgatorial state,[29] Both Origen and Gregory of Nyssa hoped that all creatures would be saved.[30] The word was still very flexible at that time, but in the mid-6th century it became virtually a technical term referring, as usually today, to a specifically Origenistic doctrine of universal salvation.[31] Maximus the Confessor outlined God's plan for "universal" salvation alongside warnings of everlasting punishment for the wicked.[32]"
(Wikipedia[41])

41

The apocatastasis, is a human philosophy, an invention of man which teaches in the end God will restore to its original design creation, including Satan and evil spirits. However, the Scriptures simply teach the final state of Satan and evil spirits is the Lake of Fire, for all eternity. God judgment upon Satan is "not redeemable," Satan can never be recovered from his rebellion to God. The doctrine which ties Universal Salvation
with the redemption of Satan and evil spirits was condemned by Church councils as heretical.

"The term apocatastasis is mentioned in the 14th of the 15 anathemas against Origen of 553: "If anyone shall say ... that in this pretended apocatastasis, spirits only will continue to exist, as it was in the feigned pre-existence: let him be anathema."[22]

A form of apocatastasis was also attributed to Gregory of Nyssa[23] and possibly the Ambrosiaster, attributed to Ambrose of Milan. Gregory of Nazianzus discussed it without reaching a decision.

A local Synod of Constantinople (543) condemned a form of apocatastasis as being Anathema, and the Anathema was formally submitted to the Fifth Ecumenical Council of Constantinople (553). Since apocatastasis had been used earlier in writers commenting on Peter's use in the New Testament, the form of apocatastasis condemned in 543 and 553 was a later development." (Wikipedia)[42]

Chapter 6
The Lie of Universal Salvation

Now in contrast to the facts of Scripture is the false teaching of Universal Salvation. When the wisdom of man gets involved, often manmade philosophy is injected into the doctrines of the Bible. Just like the Catholics which attempt to save a man by purgatory, the modern Protestant Church in some cases also now wants to eliminate the everlasting punishment of Hell Fire. The false doctrine which many Protestant Christians teachers now attempt to incorporate is called Universal Salvation.

"In Christian theology, universal reconciliation (also called universal salvation, Christian universalism, or in context simply universalism) is the doctrine that all sinful and alienated human souls—because of divine love and mercy—will ultimately be reconciled to God.[1] The doctrine has generally been rejected by Christian religion, which holds to the doctrine of special salvation that only some members of humanity will eventually enter heaven, but it has received support from many prestigious Christian thinkers as well as many groups of Christians. The Bible itself has a variety of verses that, on the surface, seem to support a plurality of views.[2]

Universal salvation may be related to the perception of a problem of Hell, standing opposed to ideas such as endless conscious torment in Hell, but may also include a period of finite punishment similar to a state of purgatory.[2] Believers in universal reconciliation may support the view that while there may be a real "Hell" of some kind, it is neither a place of endless suffering nor a place where the spirits of human beings are ultimately 'annihilated' after enduring the just amount of divine retribution.[2]

The concept of reconciliation is related to the concept of salvation—i.e., salvation from spiritual and eventually physical death—such that the term "universal salvation" is functionally equivalent. Universalists espouse various theological beliefs concerning the process or state of salvation, but all adhere to the view that salvation history concludes with the reconciliation of the entire human race to God. Many adherents assert that the suffering and crucifixion of Jesus Christ constitute the mechanism that provides redemption for all humanity and atonement for all sins.

Unitarian Universalism is a religious movement which emerged in part from the Universalist Church, but it no longer holds any official doctrinal positions, being a non-creedal faith. Universal reconciliation, however, remains a popular viewpoint among many congregations and

individual believers including many that have not at all
associated with said church.

An alternative to universal reconciliation is the doctrine
of annihilationism, often in combination with Christian
conditionalism. Some Christian leaders, such as
influential theologian Martin Luther, have hypothesized
other concepts such as 'soul death'." (Wikipedia)[43]

What is Universal Salvation? It is a belief in a literal Hell,
but in the end all men in Hell will be reconciled back to
God. There are various forms of Universal Salvation
sometimes called Ultimate Reconciliation. The Universal
Salvation massage is basically God will save men out of
Hell in the end. Is this doctrine found in the Scriptures of
the Bible? The answer is absolutely not. Nowhere in
Scriptures are we told after death; the man who is not
reconciled to God can escape the eternal damnation of
God. First of all, the Bible is clear that unredeemed men
will dwell in hell. Matthew 25:46 says, Then they (the
goats)will go away to eternal punishment, but the
righteous to eternal life. According to this verse, the
punishment of the unsaved is just as eternal as the life
of the righteous. " And these shall go away into
everlasting punishment: but the righteous into life
eternal." As long as the reward of the righteous is also
as long the judgment of the unrighteous. False teachers
say Hell Fire will eventually cease to exist, but the Lord
Himself confirms that it will last forever. Matthew 25:41

and Mark 9:44 describe hell as eternal fire and unquenchable fire.

Is There Love Without Judgment

Perhaps one of the most overstated concepts about God is unconditional love. What is meant in the process of salvation, God had to accept humanity in their sinful condition acting on our behalf by dying on the Cross. Even before there was any capacity for man to receive this action of love. So, God first loved us even when we were His enemy by dying for us. This is often stated as unconditional love, God acted first to provide a way to be forgiven. However, by this action of God's love are we to assume God accepts us just as we are?

This is probably one of the most misleading statements about the love of God, "God accepts us just as we are." This is often known as the unconditional love and forgiveness of God. Did God love without condition? Is there no judgment in the love of God? Is God capable of overlooking sin and evil, and loving humanity just as we are? The answer may be surprising to many, God never over looks sin, or evil instead has judged it unto eternal judgement. In the process of eliminating all sin and evil from this present age, God has created Hell, and finally the last judgment called the Lake of Fire. Even though God loves us enough to die for us, He by no means will allow the guilty to go unpunished.

Let us break this down; "for God so loved the world, He gave us His only begotten Son, that whosoever would believe in Him should not perish but have everlasting life." (John 3:16) Look what happened, Gods love compelled Him to deal with the sins and evil in humanity. God acted on our behalf even while we were yet enemies to Him. God sent His Jesus Christ to pay the penalty for our sin, to be the Scape Goat of Gods wrath. In the love of God there is both "mercy and justice," righteousness and judgment are the foundation of Gods throne.

Simply put Gods unconditional love judged sin and pronounced a death sentence upon the corrupted sin twisted world, then died for sin of the world. Yes, God loved the world, but based upon condition, He hates our sin, and will judge a man eternally in the Lake of Fire who refuses His love and justice. God does not accept you in your sin, there is no such thing as Gods love which allows sin and wickedness to God unpunished. God did not send Christ in the world to condemn it, but to save it. However, this does not mean God lets men refuse His love. Instead, the wrath of God abides upon fallen humanity.

What is the problem with the unconditional love philosophy? Men love darkness rather than the light for their deeds are evil and will not come to the light to have their evil deeds exposed. For men hate the light... God is light too, in Him is no darkness, or sin or corruption, no love of evil. God hates sin, and His love compels Him only to do what is right and just. In the love of God, all sin is judged, condemned to eternal destruction, and all men who refuse to be saved. In this way Gods love is based completely upon His character, and nature with no capacity to love sin. This is a simple fact, no such thing as a fallen man without the wrath of God abiding upon Him. The one who loves his darkness is judged by God as a child of the devil, a child of wrath by nature.

Is this what we mean by unconditional love? Love without judgement does not exist anywhere in the whole universe. For the true character of love is to love what is holy, righteous, and good. To hate all which is corrupt and evil. For God is love, and God is light. God has both mercy and judgment.

So, do you love the darkness or the light? For even you love by condition!

John 3:14-21[44]

14 And as Moses lifted up the serpent in the wilderness, even so must the Son of man be lifted up:

15 That whosoever believeth in him should not perish, but have eternal life.

16 For God so loved the world, that he gave his only begotten Son, that whosoever believeth in himshould not perish, but have everlasting life.

17 For God sent not his Son into the world to condemn the world; but that the

---

world through him might be saved.

18 He that believeth on him is not condemned: but he that believeth not is condemned already, because he hath not believed in the name of the only begotten Son of God.

19 And this is the condemnation, that light is come into the world, and men loved darkness ratherthan light, because their deeds were evil.

20 For every one that doeth evil hateth the light, neither cometh to the light, lest his deeds should be reproved.

21 But he that doeth truth cometh to the light, that his deeds may be made manifest, that are wrought in God.

Why is the idea of eternal damnation being rejected? In modern culture the idea of a loving God who would forever damn a man in eternal torment is not readily believed. It is one thing for a literal devil and evil spirits to be punished for their crimes in a literal Hell fire, but quite another thing when modern culture presents man as basically good. A move towards rejecting the reality of Hell will in no way diminish Gods resolve to punish men there.

In the postmodern era men go to great lengths to make fallen mankind as comfortable in their sins as possible. The seeker sensitive Church has gone to great lengths to make sure visitors to Church are not offended. In this culture of catering to sin and unbelief, Hell is considered old fashioned, too harsh, bigoted, and insensitive to suit the tastes of modern thought.

Another aspect of Hell Fire thought to be intolerable is the fear produced by a never-ending suffering. A conscious awareness of the pain and torment without hope, without mercy, is just too much injustice for many Christians. What is happening is the denial of Biblical fact, just because Hell is such a frightening prospect does not mean God is unjust. The fact Hell is terrifying will not change with man's denial or sympathy.

Those who attempt to preach against eternal damnation have a flawed view of God's love. They insist a loving God could never send sinful mankind into Hells eternal damnation. Instead of denying Hell, God has made a way of escape by the Cross of Jesus Christ. A perverted view of God's love and the downplaying of sin are not the way to avoid the Biblical facts of Hell. Any man who says God is unjust for sending sinful man into an eternal fire for a lifetime of sin has never really come to understand the devastation of the fall. Sin cannot be fixed it must be destroyed, and God will not allow men to choose their love of sin and darkness without eternal consequences. In a thousand lifetimes fallen man could never overcome sin in his own ability, or his own goodness. The results would always be death, and corruption.

The modern Church has become guilty in corrupting the doctrines of eternal judgment. Manmade philosophies like Universal Salvation, or Annihilationism seduce people into believing alternative theories which deny the reality of Hell Fire, and eternal damnation.

Many contemporary pastors who do believe in the doctrine of hell consider it simply too delicate a subject to preach on. This further contributes to the modern denial of hell. Modern Christians hear little of the eternal consequences of sin, and evil spirits are more easily able to incorporate aberrant doctrines of demons in place of the authentic doctrines of the faith. Instead, Christian teachers need to contend for the faith, and not pick and choose what they approve, and disapprove according to cultural beliefs.

In reality, to contradict the teaching on eternal judgement, to modify or eliminate the Judgment of Hell is to challenge and contradict God. It is massive deception to believe man can improve upon the plan of God. So, the Church must be put into a position where you address the facts of Hell head on. So here are some questions which should be openly addressed.
1)Why does God send people to hell? The answer is simple, for sin.
The Bible says that God created hell for Satan and the wicked angels who rebelled against Him, but there are people in hell also (Matthew 25:41). Both angelic beings

and human beings are put into hell for the same reason, sin (Romans 6:23).

Gods moral perfection causes a completely righteous judgment of sin. He is entirely right in the execution not only of salvation, but His judgment of eternal damnation. God has no darkness, or moral defect so no unrighteousness is found in Him, or His judgment. Since God is eternal, immutable, and infinite, and all sins are fundamentally against God, God has decreed the just punishment for sin must also be eternal.
(Matthew 25:46).

2)There is another aspect to consider, which is that God also created the soul of man to be eternal. So, a soul which has refused Gods way of salvation will still continue to live eternally. Only eternal judgment for such a soul demonstrates the truth of righteous justice, and mercy of God.

God, therefore, has deemed all who commit sin will go to hell because they have failed to meet His righteous standard; they have broken His law of moral perfection. If God did not send people to hell for breaking His laws, it could be said that God Himself is unjust. What court of law would not convict a law breaker, or allow them to commit crimes without punishment? However, God is both just and merciful, He has made a way for sinners to avoid eternal damnation by the shed blood of the Lamb, Jesus Christ. Because of the blood sacrifice sin is still punished in His Son, and the justice and righteousness of God upheld.

Now we have determined God is just in sending men to Hell, who will go to Hell? The answer might surprise many, we all deserve the judgment of Hell. Originally Hell was created for the devil and his angels (Matthew 25:41). However, because every human being is a sinner every person past the age of accountability has already been condemned to hell (Romans 3:10; 5:12; John 3:18). We all deserve hell as the just punishment for our rebellion against God (Romans 6:23).

Jesus Christ is clear, all have sinned, and deserving of eternal punishment. Jesus Christ was also clear that Hell is an eternal punishment for those who do not obey Him (Matthew 25:46). Second Thessalonians 1:8–9 says that in the end God will punish those who do not know God and do not obey the gospel of our Lord Jesus. They will be punished with everlasting destruction and shut out from the presence of the Lord and from the glory of his might. John the Baptist said about Jesus, His winnowing fork is in his hand, and he will clear his threshing floor, gathering his wheat into the barn and burning up the chaff with unquenchable fire. (Matthew 3:12). The witness of Scriptures is all who have sinned are deserving of Hell and eternal punishment.

However, God has provided a way of escape. "Whoever believes in him is not condemned, but whoever does

not believe stands condemned already because they have not believed in the name of God's one and only Son."
(John 3:18)[45]
3)The answer is simple, those who go to hell are specifically those who do not believe in Jesus, those who refuse Jesus Christ. Instead of going to Hell, God desires eternal salvation for every person. Jesus Christ by the Cross already paid the price for our salvation, but we must accept that gift of salvation and surrender to the Lordship, the ownership of our lives to Him.
(Luke 9:23).

Chapter 7
Why Fallen Man Deserves Hell

What Is the problem of Hell according to the Judo/Christian religious tradition? Hell is viewed as Gods ultimate punishment.
"In ancient Jewish belief, the dead were consigned to Sheol, a place to which all were sent indiscriminately (cf. Genesis 37:35; Numbers 16:30-33; Psalm 86:13; Ecclesiastes 9:10). Sheol was thought of as a place situated below the ground (cf. Ezek. 31:15), a place of darkness, silence and forgetfulness (cf. Job 10:21).[4] By the third to second century BC, the idea had grown to encompass separate divisions in sheol for the righteous and wicked (cf. the Book of Enoch),[5] and by the time of Jesus, some Jews had come to believe that those in

---

Sheol awaited the resurrection of the dead either in comfort (in the bosom of Abraham) or in torment. By at least the late rabbinical period, Gehenna was viewed as the place of ultimate punishment, exemplified by the rabbinical statement "the best of physicians are destined to Gehenna." (M. Kiddushin 4:14); also described in Assumption of Moses and 2 Esdras.[6] The term is derived from ge-hinnom, a valley near Jerusalem originally used as a location for human sacrifices to the idol Moloch." (Wikipedia)[46]

How can Christians reconcile a God who would send His Son Jesus Christ to die on the Cross to reconcile the world unto Himself, then justify eternal wrath upon those who refuse His salvation? Hell, then deals with the issue of original sin, the curse of God, and eternal judgment.

Hell's mouth is being enlarged as the souls of fallen man is filling up God's eternal judgment. In truth more die and go to hell everyday under the curse of sin and death, than come to saving faith. In Hell fire fallen man has lost all hope of mercy being born a natural enemy of God. Alienated from birth, a twisted God hating child of wrath. Resisting God's appeal all their lives, blaming and cursing God all the way to Hell. Now tell me does the modern Church agree with God's judgment on original sin.

46

Romans 3:10-18[47]

10 As it is written, There is none righteous, no, not one:
11 There is none that understandeth, there is none that seeketh after God.
12 They are all gone out of the way, they are together become unprofitable; there is none that doeth good, no, not one.
13 Their throat is an open sepulchre; with their tongues they have used deceit; the poison of asps is under their lips:
14 Whose mouth is full of cursing and bitterness:
15 Their feet are swift to shed blood:
16 Destruction and misery are in their ways:
17 And the way of peace have they not known:
18 There is no fear of God before their eyes.

Original Sin: Hatred of God.

Perhaps the Church has forgotten how far removed from God original sin has positioned fallen man. We must not forget how corrupted Adam became in falling into the sin nature, completely transforming him into a natural enemy of God. At one time mankind was created after the image and likeness of God, but now original sin has made him a child of wrath, a son of Satan. Let us look at the words of Jesus Christ in describing the results of original sin:
1) God Is Not their Father
2) Cannot Hear the Word of God
3) Satan Is Their Father

---

[47]

4) Do by Nature the Lusts of Satan
5) Lies and Deception
6) Rebel Against the Truth

" Jesus said unto them, If God were your Father, ye would love me: for I proceeded forth and came from God; neither came I of myself, but he sent me. Why Ye not understand my speech? even because ye cannot hear my word. Ye are of your father the devil, and Lusts of your father ye will do. He was a murderer from the beginning, and abode not in the truth, because there is no truth in him. When he speaketh a lie, he speaketh of his own: for he is a liar, and the father of it. And because I tell you the truth, ye believe me not. Which of you convinceth me of sin? And if I say the truth, why do ye not believe me? Is of God and heareth God's words: ye therefore hear them not, because ye are not of God." (John 8:42-47)[48]

Now Jesus Christ makes it clear men in the condition of original sin are God hating and love the darkness. Instead of the nature of God are children of a twisted corrupted sin nature committed to destroy Jesus Christ. Like Satan who was a liar and murderer from the very first act in the Garden of Eden. So instead of seeking out the presence of God and seeking out the truth are natural rebels against God who suppress the truth in unrighteousness.

48

Now what does man in original sin have to do in order to be a child of Satan who hates God? The answer is simple, just be born into this present evil age born with a corrupted sin nature inherited from original sin. All a man has to do in order to hate God is born into this world. If you want to really understand this truth just see what happened to Jesus Christ when He walked as a man. Jesus Christ the only begotten Son of God, a perfect man without sin was hated by sinful man without cause. Why did men want to destroy Jesus Christ? " All men stand guilty before God condemned in their sin. Jesus Christ exposed and convicted them of their sin. Then Jesus said unto them, my time is not yet come but your time is alway ready. The world cannot hate you; but me it hateth, because I testify of it, that the works thereof are evil."
(John 7:6-7)[49]

Why does mankind want to destroy Jesus Christ, they love darkness rather than the light because their deeds are evil, and Jesus Christ testifies of their evil deeds. Now is man in original sin born good, God loving and God seeking able to hear the Words of God and respond in repentance being exposed in their wickedness? How utterly corrupted is man in original sin, without goodness, sin loving God hating child of wrath. What is the outcome of natural man who hates God all his life? He dies under the wrath of God and awakes in the fires of Hell being incarcerated under the judgment of God.

49

Why did God make Hell and why is Hell being enlarged on a daily basis? " The wicked shall be turned into hell, and all the nations that forget God." (Psalm 9:17)[50]

What a false picture the Church has given to modern man born in original sin. Not warning them of their natural hatred of God, a child of wrath, and eternal judgment in the Lake of Fire. Instead, we deceive them with smooth speech fearing we will offend their sensibilities. Deceiving them with false peace somehow God's has changed His mind and will no longer condemn their evil deeds. How sophisticated the modern Church has become in seeker sensitivity removing all offense of the gospel, no more judgment, no more hell, just heaven and a generic god of love. Hell must enlarge her mouth as all the dignified men of culture, fame, and fortune die in their original sin and go to hell.

Isaiah 5:14-16[51]
14 Therefore hell hath enlarged herself and opened her mouth without measure: and their glory, and their multitude, and their pomp, and he that rejoiceth, shall descend into it.
15 And the mean man shall be brought down, and the mighty man shall be humbled, and the eyes of the lofty shall be humbled:
16 But the Lord of hosts shall be exalted in judgment, and God that is holy shall be sanctified in righteousness.

50
51

Gods Wrath and Ultimate Judgment

How can anyone understand the depths of Gods judgment until they see the warnings of Gods wrath. In these days' judgment is not allowed in the typical Church, so Christians rarely get a fair chance to see this part of Gods nature. In fact, many in the modern Church refuse the testimony of history, and of Scriptures and teach in the end all men will be saved. The concept of wrath and eternal judgment are being systematically eliminated by the false doctrine all mankind will be in end saved out of Hell. (Universal Salvation)

The modern belief is the love of God is what saves us, and even in Hell the fire is the love of God not the fire of His wrath. All this seems empathetic to man's mind in order not to offend modern culture with the teaching men suffer the wrath of God in Hell. However, Church history and the Scriptures tell us the real truth about Gods wrath. In the true depiction of Gods nature not only is their mercy and grace as demonstrated by the Cross of Jesus Christ. There is also Hell, and the Lake of Fire to satisfy Gods judicial nature, and His wrath.

When the apostle Peter wants to warn us about the depths of God's eternal judgment, the true nature of His wrath three examples is used to warn us. 1) The Deepest Hell Is Tartarus where the fallen angels from Noah's day are chained in everlasting darkness. 2) The worldwide catastrophic flood in the days of Noah, which destroyed every man on the face of the earth except Noah and his family. 3) The fire and brimstone which fell from heaven to destroy the entire city and population of Sodom, while saving only Lot and his wife and two daughters.

What does these stories demonstrate? God has had ultimate judgment in which there was no point of return. God has fury, God has wrath. What is the point of His judgment, God will give ample opportunity for mankind to turn from the sin and rebellion? However, there comes a point when mercy and grace have long passed, and Gods wrath is poured out without remedy. God has warned the fallen angels are all doomed to eternal fire. His example, a part of the angels who did not fall in the original rebellion with Satan, instead left the first estate during the days of Noah. The angels interacted with humans in an unlawful manner. The judgment was to chain them in the lowest Hell in chains of darkness in the portion of Hades called Tartarus. In these ways God demonstrates the reality of Hell, and the final judgments which will come upon all the fallen angels at the end of this present evil age. Satan and his dark angels will be cast into the Lake of Fire, as the wrath of God will burn against them for all eternity.

The wrath of God in the great flood of Noah's day, demonstrates how God destroyed all mankind in those days without any chance of mercy. This is a foreshadowing of the final judgment yet to come at the end of this present evil age. In the final years before the Second Coming of Jesus Christ, Gods wrath will be being poured out in fiery judgments. Before this massive loss of humanity in catastrophic judgment, the whole world will display an attitude like the days of Noah. In the Days of Noah, the fear of the Lord had completely departed. Like in the Days of Noah the world will be filled with violence and the thought of man will be continually evil not knowing the days of Gods wrath will soon pour out upon them. We can see from the Book of Revelation, just like massive loss of life in the days of Noah so will be the final acts of judgment in the days of Gods wrath. Sadly, mankind is being blinded how close these days are drawing near.

Genesis 6:5-8[52]
5 And God saw that the wickedness of man was great in the earth, and that every imagination of the thoughts of his heart was only evil continually.
6 And it repented the Lord that he had made man on the earth, and it grieved him at his heart.
7 And the Lord said, I will destroy man whom I have created from the face of the earth; both man, and beast, and the creeping thing, and the fowls of the air; for it repenteth me that I have made them.
8 But Noah found grace in the eyes of the Lord.

52

Finally, the fire and brimstone judgment of God upon Sodom is given as an example of Gods wrath. What is this example all about? How culture can depart entirely from the morality of God and live in perverse rebellious lives. Feeding on sexual sin without any fear of consequences. Why does mankind refuse the record of eternal judgment? The reality of Hell Fire and the Lake of Fire?

Sin has seared their conscience to the point where God has given over to a reprobate mind. One of the realities God has given mankind over to a reprobate life, is the pervasive presence of sexual perversity. Are not these attitudes being now celebrated and displayed in our days? Men love their darkness and hate the light will God then save them by His love, when they hate God and rebel against His creation in sexual perversity? In the final judgments, the fire of God's judgment is poured out as in the days of Sodom. Also like the days of Sodom mankind will celebrate sexual perversity, and exchange what God has created for what is against His creation. (Homosexuality).
Heed Peters warning. The days of burning the earth are just ahead. Also, mankind will mock Gods wrath saying where is the promise of His coming? No fear of God will exist upon the earth, except in a few individuals who are like Noah, and Lot. God knows how to deliver the Godly out of temptations and reserve the unjust for the day of His wrath.

2 Peter 2:4-9[53]
4 For if God spared not the angels that sinned, but cast them down to hell, and delivered them into chains of darkness, to be reserved unto judgment.
5 And spared not the old world, but saved Noah the eighth person, a preacher of righteousness, bringing in the flood upon the world of the ungodly.
6 And turning the cities of Sodom and Gomorrha into ashes condemned them with an overthrow, making them an ensample unto those that after should live ungodly.
7 And delivered just Lot, vexed with the filthy conversation of the wicked:
8 (For that righteous man dwelling among them, in seeing and hearing, vexed his righteous soul from day to day with their unlawful deeds;)
9 The Lord knoweth how to deliver the godly out of temptations, and to reserve the unjust unto the day of judgment to be punished:

2 Peter 3:2-15[54]
2 That ye may be mindful of the words which were spoken before by the holy prophets, and of the commandment of us the apostles of the Lord and Saviour:
3 Knowing this first, that there shall come in the last days scoffers, walking after their own lusts,

---

53
54

4 And saying, where is the promise of his coming? for since the fathers fell asleep, all things continue as they were from the beginning of the creation.

5 For this they willingly are ignorant of, that by the word of God the heavens were of old, and the earth standing out of the water and in the water:

6 Whereby the world that then was, being overflowed with water, perished:

7 But the heavens and the earth, which are now, by the same word are kept in store, reserved unto fire against the day of judgment and perdition of ungodly men.

8 But, beloved, be not ignorant of this one thing, that one day is with the Lord as a thousand years, and a thousand years as one day.

9 The Lord is not slack concerning his promise, as some men count slackness; but is longsuffering to us-ward, not willing that any should perish, but that all should kept in store come to repentance.

10 But the day of the Lord will come as a thief in the night; in the which the heavens shall pass away with a great noise, and the elements shall melt with fervent heat, the earth also and the works that are therein shall be burned up.

11 Seeing then that all these things shall be dissolved, what manner of persons ought ye to be in all holy conversation and godliness,

12 Looking for and hasting unto the coming of the day of God, wherein the heavens being on fire shall be dissolved, and the elements shall melt with fervent heat?

13 Nevertheless we, according to his promise, look for new heavens and a new earth, where in dwelleth righteousness.

14 Wherefore, beloved, seeing that ye look for such things, be diligent that ye may be found of him in peace, without spot, and blameless.

15 And account that the longsuffering of our Lord is salvation; even as our beloved brother Paul also according to the wisdom given unto him hath written unto you.

Chapter 8
The Wrath of God

What is the biblical meaning of the wrath of God? Wrath is a response to injustice, Gods wrath is always holy, and always justified. As God is never unjust, all His judgments are right, pure, and true. All of Gods wrath, His vindication is completely free of evil. There is vast difference between the wrath of God and the wrath of man. Man's wrath is almost never pure being filled with hatred and sin. The wrath of God is a divine response to human sin and disobedience. The wrath of God is consistently directed towards those who do not follow His will.

The Old Testament prophets often wrote of a day in the future, the Day of Wrath. (Zephaniah 1:14-15). God's wrath against sin and disobedience is perfectly justified because His plan for mankind is holy and perfect, just as

God Himself is holy and perfect. God provided a way to gain divine favor, the Cross of Jesus which turns God's wrath away from the sinner. To reject God's perfect plan is to reject God's love, mercy, grace, and favor and incur His righteous wrath. In this way man can understand why New Testament passages teaches the wrath of God abides upon all mankind who are not redeemed.

John 3:36[55]
Whoever believes in the Son has eternal life, but whoever rejects the Son will not see life, for God's wrath remains on Him.

Once again, we see Gods judgment upon sin, and His blessing upon those who fulfill the conditions of the Blood Covenant. The Blood of Jesus Christ satisfying the wrath of God on the Cross becoming a curse for us for all who receive His substitutionary sacrifice and are redeemed from the curse. All who refuse Jesus Christ rejecting the Cross will be judged on the Day of Wrath at the Second Coming of Jesus Christ.

Romans 2:1-6[56]
1 Therefore thou art inexcusable, O man, whosoever thou art that judgest: for wherein thou judgest another, thou condemnest thyself; for thou that judgest doest the same things.

55
56

2 But we are sure that the judgment of God is according to truth against them which commit such things.
3 And thinkest thou this, O man, that judgest them which do such things, and doest the same, that thou shalt escape the judgment of God?
4 Or despisest thou the riches of his goodness and forbearance and longsuffering; not knowing that the goodness of God leadeth thee to repentance?
5 But after thy hardness and impenitent heart treasurest up unto thyself wrath against the day of wrath and revelation of the righteous judgment of God.
6 Who will render to every man according to his deeds:

Notice the division between men, those who seek to please God keeping his commandments. Those seeking from God the blessing of immortality and eternal life. In contrast to those who refuse to seek God, and rebel. Storing up unto themselves the wrath of God, and who will at His coming will reveal His wrath against all ungodliness. Also notice the way of escape is clearly the blood of Jesus Christ, the work of redemption from the Cross.

Romans 2:6-11[57]
6 Who will render to every man according to his deeds:
7 To them who by patient continuance in well doing seek for glory and honour and immortality, eternal life:

57

8 But unto them that are contentious, and do not obey the truth, but obey unrighteousness, indignation, and wrath,
9 Tribulation and anguish, upon every soul of man that doeth evil, of the Jew first, and also of the Gentile.
10 But glory, honour, and peace, to every man that worketh good, to the Jew first, and also to the Gentile:
11 For there is no respect of persons with God.
The wrath of God is an awesome and terrifying act. Those who will be justified, have been covered by the blood of Christ. Only those who are redeemed from the curse, can be assured that God's wrath will never fall on them.

Romans 5:9[58]
Since we have now been justified by His blood, how much more shall we be saved from God's wrath through Him.

Is Gods Jealousy Connected To His Wrath

It is important to understand how the word jealousy is used in the Scriptures. Its use in Exodus 20:5 is to describe Gods jealousy over the worship of idols. Gods jealousy is different from how it is used to describe mankind in the sin of jealousy (Galatians 5:20). When we use the word jealous, we use it in the sense of being envious of someone who has something we do not have. A person might be jealous or envious of another

---

58

person because he or she has a nice car or home (possessions). Or a person might be jealous or envious of another person because of some ability or skill that other person has (such as athletic ability). Another example would be that one person might be jealous or envious of another because of his or her beauty.

In Exodus 20:5, it is not that God is jealous or envious because someone has something He wants or needs. Exodus 20:4-5 says, "You shall not make for yourself an idol in the form of anything in heaven above or on the earth beneath or in the waters below. You shall not bow down to them or worship them; for I, the LORD your God, am a jealous God..." Notice that God is jealous when someone gives to another something that rightly belongs to Him.
In these verses, God is speaking of people making idols and bowing down and worshiping those idols instead of giving God the worship that belongs to Him alone. God is possessive of the worship and the glory which belongs to Him. It is a sin (as God points out in 1st and 2nd commandments) to worship or serve anything other than God. It is a sin when we desire, or we are envious, or we are jealous of someone because he has something that we do not have. It is a different use of the word jealous as when compared to when God says He is jealous. What He is jealous of belongs to Him; worship and glory belong to Him alone and are to be given to Him alone.

Perhaps a practical example will help us understand the difference. If a husband sees another man flirting with his wife, he is right to be jealous for only he has the right to flirt with his wife. This type of jealousy is not sinful. Rather, it is entirely appropriate. Being jealous for something that God declares to belong to you is good and appropriate. Jealousy is a sin when it is a desire for something that does not belong to you. Worship, praise, honor, and adoration belong to God alone for only He is truly worthy of it. Therefore, God is rightly jealous when worship, praise, honor, or adoration is given to idols. This is precisely the jealousy the apostle Paul described in 2 Corinthians 11:2, "I am jealous for you with a godly jealousy..."

Gods Fire and Judgement
In the Scriptures fire is often associated with the presence of God, like the burning bush, or Mount Sinai, or even the Pillar of Fire which led Israel in the wilderness. Fire could also be associated with Gods choosing and acceptance, like when the fire fell upon the sacrifices. However, fire from God can also be associated with His wrath and judgment.

Because of fire's heat and destructive capacity, it frequently appears in the Bible as a symbol of God's anger and of the judgment. When Scripture reveal the wrath of God, the fire of God always consumes and destroys. The wrath of God is often displayed by the prophets of Old as fire falling in judgment, or God coming down in fire. Isaiah records the battle of Armageddon as God coming down in fiery flames of rebuke. Jeremiah speaks of God wrath as fire upon the destruction of Jerusalem. Ezekiel also speaks of the fiery anger of God with the impending conquest by Babylon.

The anger of God in real life events happened in the Old Testament as a display of divine wrath and judgment. In the Sinai desert Gods anger was aroused and fire from the Lord burned among the people (Numbers 11:1). Israel's idol worship, their acts of rebellion would often draw the fire of God in judgment. Korah's rebellion and the rebellion of other leaders, also resulted in many of them perishing by fire, a manifestation of God's hot anger. (Numbers 16:35 ; 26:10 ; Leviticus 10:2).

In this example of Gods wrath, the ground opened up underneath Korah and swallowed them whole and alive directly into Hades. How dire is the judgment of God upon sinning leaders, as they responsible for influencing the reactions of others in rebellion against God? In the New Testament Korahs rebellion is used as warning against men who creep into the Church, and lead Christians into apostasy by their false doctrines and rebellion.

Jude 1:8-16[59]
8 Likewise also these filthy dreamers defile the flesh, despise dominion, and speak evil of dignities.

---

9 Yet Michael the archangel, when contending with the devil he disputed about the body of Moses, durst not bring against him a railing accusation, but said, The Lord rebuke thee.

10 But these speak evil of those things which they know not: but what they know naturally, as brute beasts, in those things they corrupt themselves.

11 Woe unto them! for they have gone in the way of Cain and ran greedily after the error of Balaam for reward and perished in the gainsaying of Core.

12 These are spots in your feasts of charity, when they feast with you, feeding themselves without fear: clouds they are without water, carried about of winds; trees whose fruit withereth, without fruit, twice dead, plucked up by the roots.

13 Raging waves of the sea, foaming out their own shame; wandering stars, to whom is reserved the blackness of darkness forever.

14 And Enoch also, the seventh from Adam, prophesied of these, saying, Behold, the Lord cometh with ten thousands of his saints,

5 To execute judgment upon all, and to convince all that are ungodly among them of all their ungodly deeds which they have ungodly committed, and of all their hard speeches which ungodly sinners have spoken against him.

16 These are murmurers, complainers, walking after their own lusts; and their mouth speaketh great swelling words, having men's persons in admiration because of advantage.

Of course, in the end the fire of Gods judgment does burn all men who refuse the redemption of the Lord. Their final lot will be the Lake of fire and eternal suffering in Gods judicial Hell Fire. In the New Testament fire is associated with the judgment of hell (Matt 3:12 ; 5:22 ; 18:8-9 ; Mark 9:43 Mark 9:48 ; Luke 3:17 ; 16:24 ; James 3:6 ; Jude 7 ; Rev 20:14-15)

What does it mean that God is a consuming fire?

God is first identified as a consuming fire in Deuteronomy 4:24, as Moses reminds curse upon their sins and idolatry. The statement then appears again in the Book of Hebrews warning Christians to worship God with reverence against the sin of apostasy. The comparison is Christians are not subjected to the Mountain which burned with fire, Mount Sinai, instead the heavenly Mount Zion. To sin the sin of apostasy will draw the judgment of God upon Christians. Where the writer of Hebrews quotes the Deuteronomy passage; our God is a consuming fire. Thereby relating the fiery judgments of God against Israel, and with Christians who are committing the sin of apostasy.

Hebrews 12:18-29[60]

---

18 For ye are not come unto the mount that might be touched, and that burned with fire, nor unto blackness, and darkness, and tempest,
19 And the sound of a trumpet, and the voice of words, which voice they that heard intreated that the word should not be spoken to them anymore:
20 (For they could not endure that which was commanded, and if so, much as a beast touch the mountain, it shall be stoned, or thrust through with a dart:
21 And so terrible was the sight, that Moses said, I exceedingly fear and quake:)
22 But ye are come unto mount Sion, and unto the city of the living God, the heavenly Jerusalem, and to an innumerable company of angels,
23 To the general assembly and church of the firstborn, which are written in heaven, and to God the Judge of all, and to the spirits of just men made perfect,
24 And to Jesus the mediator of the new covenant, and to the blood of sprinkling, that speaketh better things than that of Abel.
25 See that ye refuse not him that speaketh. For if they escaped not who refused him that spake on earth, much more shall not we escape, if we turn away from him that speaketh from heaven:
26 Whose voice then shook the earth: but now he hath promised, saying, yet once more I shake not the earth only, but also heaven.
27 And this word, yet once more, signifieth the removing of those things that are shaken, as of things

that are made, that those things which cannot be shaken may remain.
28 Wherefore we receiving a kingdom which cannot be moved, let us have grace, whereby we may serve God acceptably with reverence and godly fear:
29 For our God is a consuming fire.

God is called a consuming fire by Moses when he warns the Israelites against idolatry their sin of apostasy in the wilderness. Moses warned Israel of the history of their idol worship because God is a jealous God and will not share His glory with worthless idols. God's holiness is the reason for His being a consuming fire, and His fire burns up anything unholy. The holiness of God is that part of His nature that most separates Him from sinful man. The prophet Isaiah warned, who of us can dwell with the consuming fire? Who of us can dwell with everlasting burning?

These warnings are not just restricted to people outside of a relationship with God. As already seen Moses was warning the nation of Israel on how God would judge their idolatry and apostasy. In the end the judgments of God keep sinning Israel out of their promised land inheritance. The bodies of the unfaithful fell in the wilderness under Gods oath of exclusion. The same warning goes out for apostate Christians, God will judge and exclude you from the coming Kingdom age the result of an evil heart of unbelief in Christians departing from the living God.

Hebrews 3:7-19[61]

7 Wherefore (as the Holy Ghost saith, today if ye will hear his voice,

8 Harden not your hearts, as in the provocation, in the day of temptation in the wilderness:

9 When your fathers tempted me, proved me, and saw my works forty years.

10 Wherefore I was grieved with that generation, and said, they do alway err in their heart; and they have not known my ways.

11 So I sware in my wrath, they shall not enter into my rest.)

12 Take heed, brethren, lest there be in any of you an evil heart of unbelief, in departing from the living God.

13 But exhort one another daily, while it is called today; lest any of you be hardened through the deceitfulness of sin.

14 For we are made partakers of Christ if we hold the beginning of our confidence stedfast unto the end.

15 While it is said, today if ye will hear his voice, harden not your hearts, as in the provocation.

16 For some, when they had heard, did provoke: howbeit not all that came out of Egypt by Moses.

17 But with whom was he grieved forty years? was it not with them that had sinned, whose carcases fell in the wilderness?

18 And to whom sware he that they should not enter into his rest, but to them that believed not?

61

19 So we see that they could not enter in because of unbelief.

Can apostate Christians fall into the judgment of God by denying Jesus Christ, and turning back to their worthless idols? Israel suffered Gods oath where He swore in His wrath; "they shall not enter into My rest." Now a promise remains for us Christians of a rest and reward at the end of this age. God will give the rewards of the Millennial Kingdom to all saints who are qualified during their lifetimes of walking with God in faith. However, like faithless Israel, God will exclude all saints who depart from God by an evil heart of unbelief.

Chapter 9
Gehenna Fire

What is Gehenna? The word Gehenna is the Greek transliteration of the Hebrew ge-hinnom, meaning; Valley of sons of Hinnom. This valley south of Jerusalem was where some of the ancient Israelites worshipped foreign gods. Causing their children to be sacrificed passing them through the fire, burning them to the Canaanite god Molech (2 Chronicles 28:3; 33:6; Jeremiah 7:31; 19:2–6). The place is called "Tophet" in Isaiah 30:33. In later years, Gehenna continued to be an unclean place used for burning trash from the city of Jerusalem. Jesus used Gehenna as an illustration of Hell.

God warned about worshiping the gods of surrounding nations. In particular despised the practice of child sacrifice. Burning their children to the false god Molech. So reprehensible was that practice, God explicitly forbade the Israelites from having anything to do with this vile worship.(Leviticus 18:21). God warned Israel of His dire judgments in Molech worship. In keeping with His judgments upon idol worship, God renamed the Valley of Hinnom as the Valley of Slaughter (Jeremiah 19). In the last days Gods judgment will be fully expected against all who take the Mark of the Beast and worship the Antichrist. Surely this valley will become a valley of Slaughter when the Lord Jesus Christ returns.

In the times of Jesus Christ, the Gehenna Valley was thus a place of burning sewage and garbage. Maggots and worms crawled through the waste, and the stench of burning smoke smelled strong and sickening (Isaiah 30:33). It was a place utterly filthy, disgusting, and repulsive to the nose and eyes. Gehenna presented such a vivid image that Christ used it as a symbolic depiction of Hell. (Matthew 10:28; Mark 9:47–48).

https://www.gotquestions.org/Gehenna.html[62]

Why Did Jesus Christ Warn Disciples of Gehenna Fire?

In the synoptic Gospels Jesus uses the word Gehenna to describe the opposite to life in the Kingdom (Mark 9:43-

---

48). It is used 11 times in these accounts.[32] In certain usage, it is a place where both soul (Greek: ψυχή) and body could be destroyed (Matthew 10:28) in "unquenchable fire" (Mark 9:43).[33]

Matthew 5:22: "....whoever shall say, 'You fool,' shall be guilty enough to go into Gehenna."
Matthew 5:29: "....it is better for you that one of the parts of your body perish, than for your whole body to be thrown into Gehenna."
Matthew 5:30: "....better for you that one of the parts of your body perish, than for your whole body to go into Gehenna."
Matthew 10:28: "....rather fear Him who is able to destroy both soul [Greek: ψυχή] and body in Gehenna."
Matthew 18:9: "It is better for you to enter life with one eye, than with two eyes to be thrown into the Gehenna...."
Matthew 23:15: "Woe to you, scribes and Pharisees, hypocrites, because you... make one proselyte...twice as much a child of Gehenna as yourselves."
Matthew 23:33, to the Pharisees: "You serpents, you brood of vipers, how shall you to escape the sentence of Gehenna?"
Mark 9:43: "It is better for you to enter life crippled, than having your two hands, to go into Gehenna into the unquenchable fire."
Mark 9:45: "It is better for you to enter life lame, than having your two feet, to be cast into Gehenna."

Mark 9:47: "It is better for you to enter the Kingdom of God with one eye, than having two eyes, to be cast into Gehenna."
Luke 12:5: "....fear the One who, after He has killed has authority to cast into Gehenna; yes, I tell you, fear Him."
James is the only other writer to use the word Gehenna in the New Testament:[34]
James 3:6: "And the tongue is a fire...and sets on fire the course of our life and is set on fire by Gehenna." (Wikipedia)[63]

In Scriptures Jesus Christ even warns the disciples of Gehenna fire. So, we must consider the consequences of sinning saints at the Judgement Seat of Christ. Since Christians are the one being judged, this is a topic filled with controversy and many are unwilling to face the facts of Scriptures. So here are some simple things to look at. First it is a fact Christians will be judged at the Second Coming of Jesus Christ. The judgment is not a matter of their salvation, instead what is held in question is the testing of their works after coming into saving faith. What hangs in the balance is Kingdom age reward, or their loss. The Parables of the Talents, Pounds, and Ten Virgins all reveal the same message. Some Christians will be rewarded in the Kingdom age, others will forfeit their rewards.

The apostle Paul helps us understand the matter of Christian judgment with the judicial fires of God testing the quality of every man's works. The fire is from God, Christians the ones being tested as the fire reveals the materials, and the quality of every man's work. The fire does not test the foundation of the saint's salvation, as the fire only tests those things built upon the foundation of salvation. The judicial fire can burn up all the defective works, and the soul is still saved. Obviously, the Cross has judged the curse of sin and death, redeeming the man from eternal damnation. However, does not stop the loss of the Kingdom age rewards.

1 Corinthians 3:11-15[64]
11 For other foundation can no man lay than that is laid, which is Jesus Christ.
12 Now if any man build upon this foundation gold, silver, precious stones, wood, hay, stubble;
13 Every man's work shall be made manifest: for the day shall declare it, because it shall be revealed by fire; and the fire shall try every man's work of what sort it is.
14 If any man's work abide which he hath built thereupon, he shall receive a reward.
15 If any man's work shall be burned, he shall suffer loss: but he himself shall be saved; yet so as by fire.

It is obvious by this Scripture, the fire of testing is from God, and at the Second Coming of Jesus Christ. A Christian must pass the test of judicial fires at the

---

64

Judgment Seat of Christ to receive rewards in the Kingdom age.

Now comes the difficulty, what kind of loss of rewards can be actually experienced by Christians at the Judgment Seat? Can Christians who suffer loss experience punishment at the Second Coming? Since the fire at the Judgment Seat qualifies the Christian for rewards, not salvation. Why would punishment even come into question when the man is already eternally saved? Of course, this has been debated all the way from the false doctrine of Catholic Purgatory, and Christians being sent into Outer Darkness. Watchman Nee addresses the issue of punishment in the Kingdom drawing from the question of Christ's disciples who would be greatest in the Kingdom age.

Matthew 18:1-10
1 At the same time came the disciples unto Jesus, saying, Who is the greatest in the kingdom of heaven?
2 And Jesus called a little child unto him, and set him in the midst of them,
3 And said, Verily I say unto you, Except ye be converted, and become as little children, ye shall not enter into the kingdom of heaven.
4 Whosoever therefore shall humble himself as this little child, the same is greatest in the kingdom of heaven.
5 And whoso shall receive one such little child in my name receiveth me.

6 But whoso shall offend one of these little ones which believe in me, it were better for him that a millstone were hanged about his neck, and that he were drowned in the depth of the sea.

7 Woe unto the world because of offences! for it must needs be that offences come; but woe to that man by whom the offence cometh!

8 Wherefore if thy hand or thy foot offend thee, cut them off, and cast them from thee: it is better for thee to enter into life halt or maimed, rather than having two hands or two feet to be cast into everlasting fire.

9 And if thine eye offend thee, pluck it out, and cast it from thee: it is better for thee to enter into life with one eye, rather than having two eyes to be cast into hell fire.

10 Take heed that ye despise not one of these little ones; for I say unto you, That in heaven their angels do always behold the face of my Father which is in heaven.

THE GEHENNA OF FIRE IN THE KINGDOM
 (Excerpt from Watchman Nee)

Verses 1 through 7 are the general words of the Lord. We will just mention them briefly. We want to pay more attention to the words beginning in verse 8. The Lord Jesus expanded on this matter to point out that it is not only wrong to stumble others, but it is a serious and grave matter even to stumble yourself. Verse 8 says, "If your hand or your foot stumbles you, cut it off and cast it from you." Who does "you" refer to here? In verses 3 through 7, "you" refers to the disciples who asked the question in verse 1. After the Lord Jesus answered them, He told them to be watchful and not to stumble others. The Lord's words in verse 8 are directed at the same people. If a hand or a foot stumbles you, it is better to cut it off and cast it away. Of course, this need not be taken literally. If your hands steal and your feet walk in improper paths, that is, if there is sin and lust in you, you must deal with them. "It is better for you to enter into life maimed or lame than to have two hands or two feet and be cast into the eternal fire" (v. 8).

The Lord shows us that if Christians tolerate sin, they will suffer either the casting into the eternal fire with both hands and both feet, or the entering into life with one hand or one foot. This shows us clearly that there are those who deal with their sins and lusts in this age and who will enter into the kingdom with one hand or one foot. There are also those who will leave their lusts unchecked and will be cast into the eternal fire. The fire is an eternal fire, but it does not say that they will remain in the eternal fire forever. What the Lord Jesus did not say is as significant as what He did say. If a person has become a Christian but his hands or feet sin all the time, he will suffer the punishment of the eternal fire in the kingdom of the heavens. He will not suffer this punishment eternally but will suffer it only in the age of the kingdom.

What does it mean to cut off a hand or a foot? When a man cuts off his hand or foot, he can still sin. If he does not have a foot, he can travel by car. If one of his hands is cut off, he can still sin with the other hand. It is not necessarily the Lord's intention that we cut off a hand or foot, for even if we do cut off a hand, we still cannot remove our lust. Therefore, this word must not refer to the outward body, but to the inward lust. What we have to cut off is that which drives us to sin.

Another thing that we have to realize is that the person spoken of here must be a Christian, for only a Christian is clean in his body as a whole and can thus enter into life after dealing with his lust in a single member of his body. It would not be enough for the unbelievers to cut off a hand or a foot. Even if they were to cut off both hands and both feet, they would still have to go to hell. In order to enter the kingdom of the heavens, it is better for a Christian to have an incomplete body than to go into eternal fire because of incomplete dealing.

(Gospel of God, The (2 volume set), Chapter 24, by Watchman Nee)[65]

Watchman Nee teaches Christians can lose the Kingdom age completely and be punished like unbelievers in the Gehenna fire. Of course, this interpretation is filled with controversy as this would be similar to Catholics Purgatory. Only what is being taught is not salvation after the Second Coming, instead punishment upon the

---

65

already saved. The punishment comes from the judicial
fires of God.

which is the same fire which punishes the unbeliever in
Hell. Nee teaches Christians who fail in sanctification
and bury their talents can be punished in judicial fires as
a form of Christian discipline. A loss of the Kingdom, and
punishment, but not the loss of eternal salvation.
Other Scriptures which Paul teaches also speak of
Kingdom forfeiture. Jesus Christ in the Sermon on the
Mount also warned of Christians not being able to enter
the Kingdom age.

Matthew 7:21-23[66]
21 Not everyone that saith unto me, Lord, Lord, shall
enter into the kingdom of heaven; but he that doeth the
will of my Father which is in heaven.
22 Many will say to me in that day, Lord, Lord, have we
not prophesied in thy name? and in thy name have cast
out devils? and in thy name done many wonderful
works?
23 And then will I profess unto them, I never knew you:
depart from me, ye that work iniquity.

1 Corinthians 6:8-10 [67]
8 Nay, ye do wrong, and defraud, and that your
brethren.
9 Know ye not that the unrighteous shall not inherit the
kingdom of God? Be not deceived: neither fornicators,

---

[66]
[67]

nor idolaters, nor adulterers, nor effeminate, nor abusers of themselves with mankind,
10 Nor thieves, nor covetous, nor drunkards, nor revilers, nor extortioners, shall inherit the kingdom of God.

Ephesians 5:1-7[68]
1 Be ye therefore followers of God, as dear children.
2 And walk-in love, as Christ also hath loved us, and hath given himself for us an offering and a sacrifice to God for a sweet smelling savour.
3 But fornication, and all uncleanness, or covetousness, let it not be once named among you, as becometh saints.
4 Neither filthiness, nor foolish talking, nor jesting, which are not convenient: but rather giving of thanks.
5 For this ye know, that no whoremonger, nor unclean person, nor covetous man, who is an idolater, hath any inheritance in the kingdom of Christ and of God.
6 Let no man deceive you with vain words: for because of these things cometh the wrath of God upon the children of disobedience.
7 Be not ye therefore partakers with them.

Galatians 5:19-21[69]
19 Now the works of the flesh are manifest, which are these, Adultery, fornication, uncleanness, lasciviousness,

---

68
69

20 Idolatry, witchcraft, hatred, variance, emulations, wrath, strife, seditions, heresies,
21 Envyings, murders, drunkenness, revellings, and such like: of the which I tell you before, as I have also told you in time past, that they which do such things shall not inherit the kingdom of God.

All these Scriptural passages warn Christians of Kingdom loss because of their lawless deeds. So, the only real debate among Christians who lose the Kingdom of Heaven age, is if they lose their salvation too? Kingdom loss is a fact of Scripture, but are Christians losing their salvation a fact of Scriptures? Many Christian teachers will just say those who lose the Kingdom were never really born again in the first place. However, this is not a real argument as the Judgment Seat judgment is for Christians only, no unbelievers will appear to be judged for their works. Watchman Nee and others teach the loss of the Kingdom only, while maintaining eternal salvation.

The next question which should be examined; can Christians maintain their salvation, and yet experience punishment at the Second Coming? Once again, the Catholic Church teaches Purgatory a false doctrine. Purgatory teaches salvation after men die, the Scriptures of the Bible do not. However, does the Bible teach punishment as a form of discipline for already saved Christians at the Second Coming? Here is additional Scriptural evidence which points to this possibility.

Luke 12:36-48[70]

36 And ye yourselves like unto men that wait for their lord, when he will return from the wedding; that when he cometh and knocketh, they may open unto him immediately.

37 Blessed are those servants, whom the lord when he cometh shall find watching: verily I say unto you, that he shall gird himself, and make them to sit down to meat, and will come forth and serve them.

38 And if he shall come in the second watch, or come in the third watch, and find them so, blessed are those servants.

39 And this know, that if the goodman of the house had known what hour the thief would come, he would have watched, and not have suffered his house to be broken through.

40 Be ye therefore ready also: for the Son of man cometh at an hour when ye think not.

41 Then Peter said unto him, Lord, speakest thou this parable unto us, or even to all?

42 And the Lord said, who then is that faithful and wise steward, whom his lord shall make ruler over his household, to give them their portion of meat in due season?

43 Blessed is that servant, whom his lord when he cometh shall find so doing.

44 Of a truth I say unto you, that he will make him ruler over all that he hath.

70

45 But and if that servant says in his heart, My lord delayeth his coming; and shall begin to beat the menservants and maidens, and to eat and drink, and to be drunken.

46 The lord of that servant will come in a day when he looketh not for him, and at an hour when he is not aware, and will cut him in sunder, and will appoint him his portion with the unbelievers.

47 And that servant, which knew his lord's will, and prepared not himself, neither did according to his will, shall be beaten with many stripes.

48 But he that knew not, and did commit things worthy of stripes, shall be beaten with few stripes. For unto whomsoever much is given, of him shall be much required: and to whom men have committed much, of him they will ask the more.

What are some important facts of these Scriptural passages?

1) They are all addressed as the servants of the Lord.
2) The one who will not prepare himself for the coming of the Lord says, My Lord delays His coming.
3) The Lord cuts in half the unfaithful servant, after the Second Coming
4) Peter asks if this Parable applies to them also.
5) The unfaithful servant is appointed with the unbelievers.

6) Another who did not fully prepare is beaten with many stripes, at the Second Coming of the Lord

7) Another unprepared is beaten with few stripes.

8) All of which demonstrate punishment as corrective discipline at the Second Coming of Jesus Christ.

All these Scriptures do point to the fact of some kind of loss at the Judgment Seat of Christ for Christians who did not live right, also did not watch and pray being unprepared for the Second Coming of the Lord. So, what does ultimate punishment of saints look like at the Judgment Seat?

"In the age of the kingdom, some Christians will receive a reward in the kingdom. Some will receive a great reward; others will receive a small reward.

Those who will not receive a reward are also divided into a few categories. One group will not enter into the kingdom at all. The Bible does not tell us where they will go. It only says that they will be kept outside the kingdom in the outer darkness (Matt. 8:12; 22:13; 25:30; Luke 13:28). They will be left outside the glory of God. Second, there will be many who, in addition to not having worked well, have specific sins not yet dealt with. They are saved, but when they die, they still have sins which they have not repented of and dealt with. They still have the problem of sin with them. These ones will be temporarily put into the fire. They will come out only after they have paid all their debts. This will last at most until the end of the kingdom. I do not know how long this period will actually be.

There are still many things which we are not clear about concerning the future, but the Bible has shown us enough. Although there are details which we have not yet seen, we do know what the children of God will face. Some will receive a reward; some will go into corruption. Some will be put into prison, and still some will be cast into the fire and be burned.

The matter of our salvation is quite clear. When a man trusts in the Lord Jesus, both salvation and eternal life are settled for him. But after a person is saved and up until he dies, his works, that is, his failures or his victories, will determine his fate in the kingdom. Our God is a just God. On the one hand, our salvation is free, and those who believe will have eternal life. No one can overturn this fact. On the other hand, we cannot sin at will just because we have received eternal life. If we bring forth thorns and thistles, we will be burned. If the Lord Jesus cannot disassociate us from our sins and if we have not settled everything in our lives, God has no choice but to chastise us in the future. He has no choice but to cleanse us with specific punishments, so that we can be together with Him in the new heaven and new earth. God is a just God. What He has prepared is also just. Once we have seen these things, we must learn the lesson and take the warnings from God."

Watchman Nee: The Gospel of God; Volume 2; Chapter
24 Section 10 0f 13[71]

Outer Darkness
What is the outer darkness? Is it a form of punishment
for failed Christians at the Judgment Seat of Christ? Or is
it just another word used for Hell?

In Scriptures outer darkness is Gods judgment
accompanied by weeping and gnashing of teeth. This is
obvious suffering for all who partake of it, so can
Christians be judged to suffer this punishment? The
weeping describes an inner pain of the heart, mind, and
soul. A suffering so intense it is expressed by beating
the breast in an expression of immense sorrow. The
gnashing of teeth describes an outward pain of the
body. Both the physical and emotional suffering in outer
darkness speaks of incredible loss at the Judgment Seat.
Many refuse to include Christians in this suffering,
however one must argue the one who says, "my Lord
delays His coming," were never Christians in the first
place. Which violates Scriptural integrity, as the other
servants who are faithful are treated as Christians and
are rewarded by the Lord.

"Matthew 25:30 says to cast out the useless slave into
the outer darkness. Is this darkness hell? Was that
useless slave a believer? Do the believers go to hell
because of not working?

We know that all three kinds of slaves will stand before the judgment seat of Christ. The judgment seat of Christ will be in the air, where the believers will be caught up (1 Thes. 4:16-17b). Hence, these believers will be in the air, and the outer darkness will be somewhere outside. For this reason, the outer darkness will be outside the Kingdom, a judgment upon unfaithful Christians. By reading Psalm 18:9 and 11, we know that thick clouds and darkness will enclose His glory when Christ descends to the air. So, the unfaithful slave will not be cast into hell, but he will be thrown into the darkness outside of the kingdom. The unfaithful slave is a believer, however buried his talents, who will not serve the Lord ,and cannot rule with the Lord. Some Christians will be judged to the outer darkness.

"In the Parable of the Wedding Feast, Jesus speaks of judging the wedding crasher; "Bind him hand and foot and cast him into the outer darkness." Obviously, this man was not properly prepared for the Wedding Feast but tried to enter anyway. God judged this man's hypocrisy severely sending this man to outer darkness. It stands in contrast to the joyous celebration attended by those of the king's invitation. Interpreting the wedding feast as Kingdom age rewards, and outer darkness must be the place outside the Wedding Feast, the Marriage Supper of the Lamb. However, many Bible teachers simply attempt to teach outer darkness refers to hell or, more properly, the lake of fire (Matthew 8:12; 13:42; 13:50; and 25:23)."

Collected Works of Watchman Nee, The (Set 1) Vol. 07: The Christian (5)[72]

Now many Scriptures warn disciples of Jesus Christ the possibility of Kingdom forfeiture. One the one hand many Christians are comfortable teaching Christians can lose their salvation, and be condemned to Hell, just like the unredeemed. However, there seems to come a great struggle among Christians about Scriptures which speak of the loss of the Kingdom instead. Those very Scriptures which warn Christians of the possibility of failing at the Judgment Seat of Christ suffering some kind of discipline in the Kingdom age.

Christians Who Walk After the Flesh Lose the Kingdom

Christians are warned of Kingdom forfeiture by being disqualified at the Judgment Seat of Christ. The apostle Paul clearly spells this out in his letter to the Church at Galatians. Paul warns those who walk after the flesh; "shall not inherit the Kingdom of God." (Galatians 5:21)

Here are the facts, an inheritance is given when one generation passes their blessing to the next generation. So, the Kingdom of Heaven age is given as an inheritance to qualified Christians who live faithful devoted lives. As a reward, a right to rule and reign with Jesus Christ at the Second Coming. The fact is the

---

Kingdom is only given to those who have earned the right. Those Christians who disqualify themselves from inheriting the Kingdom are doing so right now, by not living right with God in this age. That is why the Kingdom is not entered upon now, as its entrance is at the first resurrection where qualified Christians are raised into immortality to rule with Christ.

Its only at the end of this age qualified saints will "inherit the Kingdom," which means "they do not yet have the Kingdom." Now popular theology wants to make a much ado about how great the Kingdom of Heaven is now, but the Scriptures prove the Kingdom is future and can be lost by disqualification. Which makes "no Christian" in the Kingdom age now, neither has any Christian already inherited the Kingdom.

Now many things in the lives of modern Christians will cause them to forfeit their future inheritance and be rejected from the Kingdom age. Here is Paul's partial list; adultery, fornication, uncleanness (perversity), and lasciviousness (lust). (Galatians 5:19) Do we not see an extraordinary amount of those who proclaim faith in Christ living in sexual sin, and are in bondage to lust? Though modern culture excuses these sins under the banner of I am in love it is still considered immoral and the Lord Jesus Christ will judge you. Shutting the door to the Kingdom age to all Christians who refuse to confess their immoral lifestyles. You shall not inherit the

Kingdom of heaven, and you are in no means in the Kingdom spiritually now.

Now what about putting other things before God? (Idolatry) What about disobedience and rebellion? What about anger, hate, bitterness, and unforgiveness? What about all the Christian factions, divisions, and fighting among other Christians? (Church wars) What about all the famous men who preach heresy and divide the Church, making for followers of their false doctrines? All these things which are normally going on in the Church world, will disqualify from the Kingdom those practitioners . So, the great men who declare themselves apostles and prophets, who have twisted and corrupted the Word of God, who say the Kingdom is now will not even be "entering the real Kingdom of heaven age."

What about all the Christians who are getting high on weed, getting drunk on alcohol, who commit abortions, who are jealous and divisive, and yet want to declare the unfailing love of God. If you are a homosexual, you are immoral, your conscience says your wrong, but culture says your right. If you are a born-again Christian, you are yielding to the flesh while you live the immoral, convictions of the world. Are you getting caught up into listening to those who will itch your ears, saying your sins are already forgiven? Or all judgment on Christians has already past, and only the love of God without judgement remains. The reason you listen to false doctrine and teachers; "you want to continue in your sins." You refuse to be confronted; you act like your being put out when your life is being called into an account.

.

If you are a preacher, do you deceive by telling men in the end all men will be saved out of Hell? You tell them what they want to hear, because the true doctrines of Christ would lose your audience and popularity. You exploit the Church for your own profit. While in hypocrisy you speak of angels, of revival, but in reality, you are covetous, and are marketing the Church. The motives are clearly seen by God, you covet the worlds riches wanting to make lots of money from your hypocritical meetings. In reality you are an extortionist, holding the Church captive by your seduction and lies. Revival is not in your heart, as you hypocritically hide your own sins, and make for appearances around your life and ministry which are inflated. You have deceived the body of Christ about the true nature of your own relationship with Jesus Christ. However, you always want to "been seen," so as to make a platform for an audience, and profit. Your own hypocrisy condemns you, but you put on a show to hide your real condition.

Will these imposters who are loved for their religious performance be given the Kingdom age? Let us make this simple; "they have their reward now." What they will hear at the Judgment Seat of Christ, "depart from Me you workers of iniquity for I never knew you." The door to the Kingdom age is shut to all whose righteousness is hypocrisy. Whose walk after coming into saving faith is after the flesh. Sadly, this is what often happens with many ministers in typical modern Christianity. Christians walking after the flesh will at the Judgment Seat be disinherited by God disqualifying them from entering the Kingdom age. "Not everyone who says to Me Lord Lord shall enter the Kingdom of heaven, but only those who do the will of My Father in Heaven." (Matthew 7:21)[73]

Galatians 5:17-21[74]
17 For the flesh lusteth against the Spirit, and the Spirit against the flesh: and these are contrary the one to the other: so that ye cannot do the things that ye would.
18 But if ye be led of the Spirit, ye are not under the law.
19 Now the works of the flesh are manifest, which are these, Adultery, fornication, uncleanness, lasciviousness,
20 Idolatry, witchcraft, hatred, variance, emulations, wrath, strife, seditions, heresies,
21 Envyings, murders, drunkenness, revellings, and such like: of the which I tell you before, as I have also told you in time past, that they which do such things shall not inherit the kingdom of God.

73
74

First Jesus Christ said, Not Everyone who says to Me Lord, Lord shall enter the Kingdom of Heaven, but only those who do the will of My Father which is in heaven. (Matthew 7:21) Which many teachers go on to say those who prophesied, and worked miracles, and cast out spirits in Jesus name were never really born again because Jesus Christ rejected them at the Judgment Seat; "depart from Me you workers of iniquity." (Matthew 7:23) They say being rejected at the Judgment Seat equals the loss of salvation? However, is it the loss of salvation, or the loss of reward? If we compare other Scriptures which warn born again Christians of losing their inheritance at the Judgment, then it would be the loss of reward.

Paul also warns Christians who practice the works of the flesh; "you shall not inherit the Kingdom of God." (Galatians 5:21) Which means you can lose something at the Second Coming of Jesus Christ, even if you are a born-again Christian. So, what are some Christians in danger of losing by their fleshly living and conduct right now? Many Christians are not afraid to say salvation can be lost, and those who live Godless lives now can still go to Hell. However, they would struggle with saying Christians would lose the inheritance of the coming Kingdom age. The Scriptures are clear, losing the Kingdom is a very real danger for faithless living in this age. Why would both Jesus Christ and apostle Paul warn of Kingdom loss if it were not possible for Christians to lose it? It is apparent the Scriptures teach the entrance into the Kingdom as a right of inheritance given to faithful saints at the end of this age.

The apostle Peter also speaks for a future inheritance for Christians. (1 Peter 1:4) Combined with a salvation ready to be revealed in the last time, which is clearly a future salvation. Now we know Peter already taught Christians are saved by the Cross, so the future reward of inheritance is given to those saved by the Blood. However, the inheritance is also by qualification, meaning not every born-again Christian will be qualified at the Judgment Seat to receive it. What is this great inheritance reserved for faithful Christians? Simply put the right for Christians to rule with Jesus Christ in the coming Kingdom of Heaven age. Will many Christians lose this right by godless living now? The answer comes through a large volume of passage which warn of Kingdom loss. Peter says it is time for Judgment to begin with the household of God. If the righteous man is scarcely saved, where will the ungodly and sinner appear? (1 Peter 4:18) Does this not demonstrate the difficulty of a future Judgment?

Peter then warns of Christians who will not walk-in sanctification, how they have become blind and have forgotten they were purged from their former way of life. Peter then warns Christians to make their calling and election sure, for if Christians do the things which are right in the sight of God, they shall never fall? Warning Christians can fall in the coming Judgment.

Then Peter concludes his teaching with the promise of future reward for the faithful. What is the reward; "an abundant entrance in the coming Kingdom of our Lord and Savior Jesus Christ."

(1 Peter 1:11) Once again the Scriptures loudly proclaim a future kingdom, and future entrance into that Kingdom.

Let us be plainly clear. If the Kingdom is future and its entrance future, which the Scriptures warn some Christians will forfeit their entrance. How can the Kingdom be now before the Second Coming, and the Judgment Seat of Christ which qualifies Christians for its entrance? How seductive is Kingdom Now philosophy? As a majority of saints simply believe themselves to be building it through their Churches and ministries right now. But whose kingdom is really being built? Mans or Gods?

2 Peter 1:4-11[75]

4 Whereby are given unto us exceeding great and precious promises: that by these ye might be partakers of the divine nature, having escaped the corruption that is in the world through lust.

5 And beside this, giving all diligence, add to your faith virtue, and to virtue knowledge.

6 And to knowledge temperance; and to temperance patience; and to patience godliness.

7 And to godliness brotherly kindness; and to brotherly kindness charity.

---

8 For if these things be in you, and abound, they make you that ye shall neither be barren nor unfruitful in the knowledge of our Lord Jesus Christ.

9 But he that lacketh these things is blind, and cannot see afar off, and hath forgotten that he was purged from his old sins.

10 Wherefore the rather, brethren, give diligence to make your calling and election sure: for if ye do these things, ye shall never fall:

11 For so an entrance shall be ministered unto you abundantly into the everlasting kingdom of our Lord and Saviour Jesus Christ.

Section III

The Curse of God

What is the definition of a curse? In both the Old Testament and New Testament there are several words which carry the meaning of curse. With the Greek, there are four or five Greek words that could be translated curse. All of these Greek words have basically the same meaning, being very clear. All Greek words mean, something despised, something that is devoted to destruction, something that is doomed. That is what it means to be cursed.

Now taking those definitions and applying what it means to be cursed by God, means God has pronounced doom or destruction. The same for Hebrew words in the Old Testament where you find the words, alah, meerah, qelalah. Hebrew words which all mean basically the very same thing, cursed to doom, cursed to destruction.

"What is the definition of anathema?"

Anathema is a Greek New Testament word from anathema, accursed or consigned to damnation or destruction. The word Anathema in modern Bible translations is usually translated as accursed, cursed, or eternally condemned. Young's Literal Translation, the American Standard Version, and the King James Version transliterate it as "anathema."

Would God curse a man for preaching a false gospel?

The word anathema is used in Galatians 1:8–9. "But though we, or an angel from heaven, should preach unto you any gospel other than that which we preached unto you, let him be anathema. As we have said before, so say I now again, if any man preacheth unto you any gospel other than that which ye received, let him be anathema." In other versions anathema is translated; eternally condemned.

This is in fact a curse placed upon a man who falsely teaches or preaches another Gospel. The responsibility of men to study to show themselves approved by God; a workman who needs not to be ashamed is of eternal importance. Will God curse a man who changes or alters the Word of God?

Revelation 22:18-19[76]
18 For I testify unto every man that heareth the words of the prophecy of this book, if any man shall add unto these things, God shall add unto him the plagues that are written in this book:
19 And if any man shall take away from the words of the book of this prophecy, God shall take away his part out of the book of life, and out of the holy city, and from the things which are written in this book.

God warns all who would alter the doctrines of Scripture adjusting the Word of God to suit their own philosophical beliefs. All who have preached a false Gospel are under the curse of God. The apostle Peter said, the false teachers are in great jeopardy of Gods judgment, warning their damnation slumbers not.

2 Peter 2:1-3[77]
1 But there were false prophets also among the people, even as there shall be false teachers among you, who privily shall bring in damnable heresies, even denying the Lord that bought them, and bring upon themselves swift destruction.
2 And many shall follow their pernicious ways; by reason of whom the way of truth shall be evil spoken of.

76
77

3 And through covetousness shall they with feigned words make merchandise of you: whose judgment now of a long time lingereth not, and their damnation slumbereth not.

Anathema is also used in conjunction with the word maranatha, a Greek word used in conjunction with the hope of Christs Second Coming.
1 Corinthians 16:22: "If anyone does not love the Lord, he is to be accursed. Maranatha expresses the hope of Christ's second coming. The meaning would be related to anyone does not love the Lord; a curse be on him.

Connected to Old Testament meanings, anathema is the Hebrew word haram or harem, here we see the severity by which God curses objects of idolatry. In the Old Testament often resulted in the total annihilation of idolatrous people or nations. When God says something is anathema, it is a curse.

Chapter 10
Curse of Sin and Death

Does God have a curse? The answer would have to be yes, God has cursed sin, and the fruit of sin and death. When God gave Adam and Eve His commandments, He prohibited them from taking fruit from the Tree of the Knowledge of Good and Evil.

Genesis 2:16-17[78]
16 And the Lord God commanded the man, saying, Of every tree of the garden thou mayest freely eat:
17 But of the tree of the knowledge of good and evil, thou shalt not eat of it: for in the day that thou eatest thereof thou shalt surely die.

Gods curse is pronounced over His broken commandments, as the fruit of its transgression results in death. The reality of Gods curse can be clearly seen in His relationship, where He gave the law of His commandments. In the Book of Deuteronomy, we can see how God reaffirms the blessings for walking in obedience and keeping His commandments. Also, the curses which will result from trespassing His commandments, so Gods curse is upon sin. In the course of giving the Law of Commandments, Israel would sin and break Gods commandments. In order to be delivered from reaping the full consequences of broken commandments, Israel must offer God His ordained Blood Sacrifices for forgiveness and cleansing.

Deuteronomy 28:1-2[79]
1 And it shall come to pass, if thou shalt hearken diligently unto the voice of the Lord thy God, to observe and to do all his commandments which I command thee this day, that the Lord thy God will set thee on high above all nations of the earth:

78
79

2 And all these blessings shall come on thee, and overtake thee, if thou shalt hearken unto the voice of the Lord thy God.

Deuteronomy 28:13-15[80]
13 And the Lord shall make thee the head, and not the tail; and thou shalt be above only, and thou shalt not be beneath; if that thou hearken unto the commandments of the Lord thy God, which I command thee this day, to observe and to do them:
14 And thou shalt not go aside from any of the words which I command thee this day, to the right hand, or to the left, to go after other gods to serve them.
15 But it shall come to pass, if thou wilt not hearken unto the voice of the Lord thy God, to observe to do all his commandments and his statutes which I command thee this day; that all these curses shall come upon thee and overtake thee.

Clearly, we can see how God has cursed sin, as it took from man all the blessings God had intended in His original creation. In the fall to original sin, God also pronounces some specific curses which are still in force even today.
God cursed the serpent for being agent of deception in the Garden, and then pronounced judgment over Satan for his lies and temptation.

80

Genesis 3:13-15[81]

13 And the Lord God said unto the woman, what is this
that thou hast done? And the woman said, the serpent
beguiled me, and I did eat.

14 And the Lord God said unto the serpent, because
thou hast done this, thou art cursed above all cattle,
and above every beast of the field; upon thy belly shalt
thou go, and dust shalt thou eat all the days of thy life:

15 And I will put enmity between thee and the woman,
and between thy seed and her seed; it shall bruise thy
head, and thou shalt bruise his heel.

In the pronouncement of curses from the fall, God
cursed the ground, childbirth, man's control over the
woman in marriage, the effects which can be readily
seen in nature today. Was God the causative agent in
cursing those results from the fall. Or was God only
explaining the results of the fall, and the resulting curses
from the law of sin and death?

Genesis 3:16-19[82]

16 Unto the woman he said, I will greatly multiply thy
sorrow and thy conception; in sorrow thou shalt bring
forth children; and thy desire shall be to thy husband,
and he shall rule over thee.

17 And unto Adam he said, because thou hast
hearkened unto the voice of thy wife, and hast eaten of
the tree, of which I commanded thee, saying, Thou shalt

81

82

not eat of it: cursed is the ground for thy sake; in sorrow shalt thou eat of it all the days of thy life.
18 Thorns also and thistles shall it bring forth to thee; and thou shalt eat the herb of the field.
19 In the sweat of thy face shalt thou eat bread, till thou return unto the ground; for out of it wast thou taken: for dust thou art, and unto dust shalt thou return.

One peculiarity in Gods curses or pronouncements of the fruits of the curse from the fall is the absence of one curse in particular. In Genesis chapter three is the absence of cursing the man and woman. Instead, nature, and creation, along with Satan were cursed directly, but God gave man instead the promise of redemption. Let us make this clear God has cursed sin, and its fruit of corruption and death. We can see the heart of redemption given by God in the Garden by declaring His way of escape from sin and death.

Genesis 3:21-24[83]
21 Unto Adam also and to his wife did the Lord God make coats of skins and clothed them.
22 And the Lord God said, Behold, the man is become as one of us, to know good and evil: and now, lest he put forth his hand, and take also of the tree of life, and eat, and live forever:
23 Therefore the Lord God sent him forth from the garden of Eden, to till the ground from whence he was taken.

---

[83]

24 So he drove out the man; and he placed at the east of the garden of Eden Cherubims, and a flaming sword which turned every way, to keep the way of the tree of life.

How did God move in a redemptive way in the Garden instead of cursing Adam and Eve? First God gave the promise the seed of the woman will bruise the head of the Serpent, who is Satan. How did God demonstrate His redemptive grace and mercy, by condemning sin and pronouncing His judgment upon our fallen condition? However, God then kept Adam and Eve from eating the fruit of the Tree of Life by which man would live in a sinful and fallen mortal condition forever. God drove man out of the Garden out from the Tree of Life and placed a cherubim angel with a flaming sword to guard the Tree from man eating its fruit in the fallen condition.

However, before God drove man out from the Garden, He removed the fig leaves covering, and instead provided the skins of the Blood Sacrifice. God gave the type of His blood Sacrifice, the blood of the Lamb, the way of redemption right in the Garden. When God sacrificed the life of another to provide the covering for their sin, and nakedness before God. The skins which required the shedding of blood where the prefigure of Him who would come, as the Lamb of God to take away the sin of the world, Jesus Christ. However, fallen mankind was still tempted to approve his own way of redemption before God. How by offering the work of his hands, based upon works and human merit. Fallen man has refused Gods way of Redemption by His Blood Sacrifice and has always tried to build a temple to Heaven, to be his own god. These two types of offering have run side by side for centuries and have been the line of demarcation between Gods redeemed, and Satan's counterfeit.

Why did God give Israel the Law of Commandments thousands of years after the original fall of man? This may be a surprise to many, but the Law of Commandments was given to demonstrate how exceedingly sinful fallen man really is.

Romans 7:7-13[84]
7 What shall we say then? Is the law sin? God forbid. Nay, I had not known sin, but by the law: for I had not known lust, except the law had said, Thou shalt not covet.
8 But sin, taking occasion by the commandment, wrought in me all manner of concupiscence. For without the law sin was dead.
9 For I was alive without the law once: but when the commandment came, sin revived, and I died.
10 And the commandment, which was ordained to life, I found to be unto death.
11 For sin, taking occasion by the commandment, deceived me, and by it slew me.

84

12 Wherefore the law is holy, and the commandment holy, and just, and good.
13 Was then that which is good made death unto me? God forbid. But sin, that it might appear sin, working death in me by that which is good; that sin by the commandment might become exceeding sinful.

Here is the break down, sin is in fallen man by nature makes it is impossible for fallen man to save himself or satisfy the demands of God righteous holy justice. The sin nature in fallen man is given by being related to the original man Adam, who is the federated head of all fallen humanity. The sinful Adamic nature has dominated man since the fall which has blinded man to his need for a Savior. So, God gave the Law of Commandments. The Commandment which was given was ordained to life, but instead exposed all manner of sinful lawless actions. How, because of sin in man's nature was compelled to break Gods laws. Sin taking occasion by the commandment deceived natural fallen man and slew him. Not producing a righteous holy life before God, instead manifesting man as a law breaker.

Sin by the commandment proved how exceedingly sinful fallen man really is. Now sin working in the lives of Christians who walk after the flesh, also demonstrates how exceedingly sinful. A man born again of the Holy Spirit who will not depend entirely upon Gods Spirit will end up sowing to the flesh. Christians sowing to the flesh results in the reaping of destruction.

Now the fact is the Law of Commandments leads us to
our only hope, Jesus Christ our Savior. What the law
could not do for us as it was weakened by our sinful
flesh, God did by sending us His Son in the likeness of
sinful flesh and for sin, condemned sin in the flesh. That
the righteous of the law might be fulfilled in us, who
walk not after the flesh, but after the Spirit.
(Romans 8:3-4)[85]

Law of Commandments Our Tutor To Christ

Gods redemptive plan came by the blood Sacrifice, by
the promises of God given to Abraham the Father of the
faith. Through Abrahams seed would come the Savior of
the World, God promised redemption to Abraham by
covenant. Four Hundred thirty years later God gave the
Law of Commandments by Moses to Israel. Why did
God give the Law, it was added because of the
transgressions, a way to give forgiveness for sinful
Israel. Until the time of actual fulfilment of those
covenantal promises by the Mediator. Jesus Christ is the
promised seed of Abraham and fulfilled the conditions
of the blood Covenant by His sacrificial death on the
Cross.

Is the law against the covenantal promises of God?
More specifically, is the law against the promise of

85

redemption from sin and death, given to Abraham and his Seed (Jesus Christ) by covenant? God forbid, if the law could give us our redemptive life, then right standing before God, and right living (righteous holy) would have been by the law. However, instead the law revealed how exceedingly sinful fallen man really is. So, before the coming of Christ, the law with its commandments and sacrifices were a type, a shadow of the reality of Him who was to come, Jesus Christ.

The Law was given as our trainer to led us to faith in Jesus Christ. Scriptures reveal Gods redemption was given by promise, the promised redemption by the Blood Covenant. From the Garden, God gave Adam the pattern of the shedding of blood for the forgiveness of sin. The skins which covered Adam came from the blood sacrifice, a prefigure of the Cross, and a type of the Lamb of God who takes away the sins of the world, Jesus Christ. With Abraham, God made promise of redemption given by covenant to Abraham and his seed. The promise is understood to be the Abrahamic Covenant, Gods promise of redemption through the family line of Abraham, and his seed, Jesus Christ.

Now the Law of Commandments came four hundred thirty years after the Abrahamic Covenant cannot make void, or disannul the promise given by God to Abraham. So, what then serves the purpose of the Law of Commandments? It was given to Israel because of their sins, as a means of sacrificial forgiveness (animal sacrifices), until the time of Jesus Christ, Abrahams seed should come to who the promise was made.

Now Moses is a type of Christ, a mediator between God and man to whom the Law of Commandments was given. So, the law provided a mediatory system of priests and animal sacrifices to atone for the sins of Israel. The Law provided a way which God could dwell with His covenantal people and lead them over their enemies and to possess their inheritance. Of course, the ultimate inheritance would be life over death requiring the resurrection of the dead in order for the saints of old to possess their promises from God. The Law failed to give Israel this immortality, instead a temporary means until the Christ would come with resurrection power and eternal life.

Is the Law against the promises of God? No, the Law is holy, just, and good, it was man who was sold under the bondage of sin from the Adamic inheritance who could not fulfill the righteous requirement of the law. Instead, Israel became exceedingly sinful, as well as the rest of the whole human race of fallen man.

The law could not give Adamic man the inheritance of life over sin. For if a law could have been given which could have given life, then righteousness freedom from sin and death would have come by the law. However, the law proved man in his fallen sinful state was incapable of living a righteous holy life. Scriptures have concluded all men under sin, so the promise of redemption in Jesus Christ might be given to them who believe.

So, the Law of Commandments then proved to by our trainer, our tutor, our school master, to bring us to the only man who has ever kept the Law without even one single sin. In Jesus Christ is provided the life of righteousness, a Lamb without spot, or sin, no defect whose sinless perfection becomes the sacrifice for the sin of the world. After we understand by the works of the Law no man will be justified in the sight of God. We can have faith in Jesus Christ alone, so we are justified in the eyes of God from which the works of the law could never justify us. In this way our ultimate redemption will be accomplished. As all who have put their faith in Christ will inherit immortality and eternal life.

Galatians 3:18-25[86]
18 For if the inheritance be of the law, it is no more of promise: but God gave it to Abraham by promise.
19 Wherefore then serveth the law? It was added because of transgressions, till the seed should come to whom the promise was made; and it was ordained by angels in the hand of a mediator.
20 Now a mediator is not a mediator of one, but God is one.
21 Is the law then against the promises of God? God forbid for if there had been a law given which could

---

86

have given life, verily righteousness should have been
by the law.

22 But the scripture hath concluded all under sin, that
the promise by faith of Jesus Christ might be given to
them that believe.

23 But before faith came, we were kept under the law,
shut up unto the faith which should afterwards be
revealed.

24 Wherefore the law was our schoolmaster to bring us
unto Christ, that we might be justified by faith.

25 But after that faith is come, we are no longer under a
schoolmaster.

Chapter 11
Redeemed From The Curse
We can now understand how Jesus Christ has redeemed
us from the curse of the Law. The nation of Israel was
given the Law, with the statement of promised blessings
from God for obedience, and the dire warning of Gods
curses for transgression, and disobedience. Of course, if
Israel committed transgression of the Law, they could
seek forgiveness and cleansing by offering a sacrifice for
sin. However, sinful Israel would fall into apostasy
rebelling against the Law and God. In the end Israel's
apostasy brought upon them the curses of the Law, and
complete destruction of the nation, as promised in the
curse of the Law.

Deuteronomy 29:20-29[87]

87

20 The Lord will not spare him, but then the anger of the Lord and his jealousy shall smoke against that man, and all the curses that are written in this book shall lie upon him, and the Lord shall blot out his name from under heaven.

21 And the Lord shall separate him unto evil out of all the tribes of Israel, according to all the curses of the covenant that are written in this book of the law:

22 So that the generation to come of your children that shall rise up after you, and the stranger that shall come from a far land, shall say, when they see the plagues of that land, and the sicknesses which the Lord hath laid upon it.

23 And that the whole land thereof is brimstone, and salt, and burning, that it is not sown, nor beareth, nor any grass groweth therein, like the overthrow of Sodom, and Gomorrah, Admah, and Zeboim, which the Lord overthrew in his anger, and in his wrath:

24 Even all nations shall say, Wherefore hath the Lord done thus unto this land? what meaneth the heat of this great anger?

25 Then men shall say, Because they have forsaken the covenant of the Lord God of their fathers, which he made with them when he brought them forth out of the land of Egypt:

26 For they went and served other gods, and worshipped them, gods whom they knew not, and whom he had not given unto them:

27 And the anger of the Lord was kindled against this land, to bring upon it all the curses that are written in this book:

28 And the Lord rooted them out of their land in anger, and in wrath, and in great indignation, and cast them into another land, as it is this day.

29 The secret things belong unto the Lord our God: but those things which are revealed belong unto us and to our children forever, that we may do all the words of this law.

We can see the complete picture now of redemption. God established His Covenant of Redemption with Abraham and his seed, Jesus Christ. Abraham believed God would fulfill His promised inheritance of a redeemed humanity, and removal of the curse of sin and death. God demonstrated His promise to Abraham by making covenant, and Abraham believed God and it was accounted to Him for righteousness. Faith in the Blood Covenant makes way for the true children of God. The Blood of Jesus Christ has delivered the promises of God for all who are born again of the Holy Spirit, and who are promised full redemption. Until the Day of Redemption, their deliverance from their mortal bodies which are now kept by the sealing with the promised Holy Spirit.

God had promised Abraham in his seed would all the nations be blessed. A promise which includes all the Gentile nations, and not only the nation of Israel. So those who be of faith both Jew and Gentile are able to partake of the Abrahamic Covenant. They are blessed with faithful Abraham who now in the state of death in Paradise is awaiting his resurrection out from among the dead.

Now the curse of the Law must be dealt with in order for the nations of the earth to be blessed. As God has concluded every man an inheritor of Adamic sin, or original sin. God has cursed sin, and under the Law, it has become the Law of Sin and death. For as many as are of the works of the Law are under the curse; for it is written, cursed is everyone (any man) that continues not in all things which are written in the Book of the Law to do them.

In other words, to break the commandments of the Law makes a man a transgressor, and God has cursed sin. Let us do the math, any man which attempts to justify himself in the sight of the God apart from Jesus Christ are guilty of transgression, a law breaker. Guilty of sin and sentenced to the curse of sin and death. But that no man is justified by the law in the sight of God it is evident for all men have sinned. Are deserving of the curse of sin and death.

Let us get this right, no man outside of the Blood Covenant, the Sin Sacrifice of Jesus Christ will be given redemption, and the inheritance of immortality and eternal life. For all who offer their works, the works of the Law are under the curse. For men are incapable of perfectly keeping the law and come under its curse. Cursed is everyone who continues not in all things written in the book of the Law, not just one or two things. No man is justified in the sight of God by his own works (keeping of the Law), as all mankind has sinned and fallen short of the glory of God.

Galatians 3:6-14[88]

6 Even as Abraham believed God, and it was accounted to him for righteousness.

7 Know ye therefore that they which are of faith, the same are the children of Abraham.

8 And the scripture, foreseeing that God would justify the heathen through faith, preached before the gospel unto Abraham, saying, In thee shall all nations be blessed.

9 So then they which be of faith are blessed with faithful Abraham.

10 For as many as are of the works of the law are under the curse: for it is written, Cursed is everyone that continueth not in all things which are written in the book of the law to do them.

11 But that no man is justified by the law in the sight of God, it is evident: for, The just shall live by faith.

12 And the law is not of faith: but The man that doeth them shall live in them.

Christ Made A Curse

88

The picture of the Christ on the Cross is a picture of the cursed man of sin. In becoming our Sin Sacrifice, Jesus Christ was made a curse for us. Let us get the picture, cursed is every man who hangs on a tree. Fallen man is under the curse for sin. In the case of Jesus Christ, He who knew no sin was made to be sin for us, that we might be made the righteousness of God in Him. Jesus Christ the sinless Son of God was made to be redemption from the curse, as He hung on the Cross. The Cross of Jesus Christ is proof positive all mankind are under the curse of sin and death, and the Blood of Christ makes payment for our redemption from the curse.

Galatians 3:13-14[89]
13 Christ hath redeemed us from the curse of the law, being made a curse for us: for it is written, Cursed is every one that hangeth on a tree:
14 That the blessing of Abraham might come on the Gentiles through Jesus Christ; that we might receive the promise of the Spirit through faith.

"Let us go farther into this truth of God. How was Christ made a curse? In the first place, He was made a curse because all the sins of His people were actually laid on Him. Remember the words of the apostle—it is no doctrine of mine, mark you, it is an inspired sentence, it is God's doctrine—"He made Him to be sin for us." And let me note another passage from the prophet Isaiah,

---

89

"The Lord has laid on Him the iniquity of us all"; and yet another from the same prophet, "He shall bear their iniquities." The sins of God's people were lifted from off them, and imputed to Christ, and their sins were looked upon as if Christ had committed them! He was regarded as if He had been the sinner; He actually and in very deed stood in the sinner's place. Next to the imputation of sin came the curse of sin. The law, looking for sin to punish, with its quick eye detected sin laid upon Christ, and as it must curse sin wherever it was found, it cursed the sin as it was laid on Christ; so, Christ was made a curse. Amazing and awful words, but as they are Scriptural words, we must receive them. Sin being on Christ, the curse came on Christ, and in consequence our Lord felt an unutterable horror of soul; surely it was that horror which made Him sweat great drops of blood when He saw and felt that God was beginning to treat Him as if He had been a sinner; the holy soul of Christ shrunk with deepest agony from the slightest contact with sin, so pure and perfect was our Lord that never an evil thought had crossed His mind, nor had His soul been stained by the glances of evil. And yet He stood in God's sight, a sinner, and therefore a solemn horror fell upon His soul. The heart refused its healthful action, and a bloody sweat bedewed His face; then He began to be made a curse for us, nor did He cease till He had suffered all the penalty which was due on our account. We have been accustomed in divinity to divide the penalty into two parts, the penal- ty of loss, and the penalty of actual suffering. Christ endured both of these. It was due to sinners that they should lose God's favor and presence, and therefore Jesus cried, "My God, My God, why have You forsaken Me?" It was due to sinners that they should lose all personal comfort; Christ was deprived of every consolation, and even the last rag of clothing was torn from Him, and He was left like Adam, naked and forlorn. It was necessary that the soul should lose everything that could sustain it, and so did Christ lose every comfortable thing. He looked, and there was no man to pity or help; He was made to cry, "But I am a worm and no man; a reproach of men and despised of the people."

As for the second part of the punishment, namely, an actual infliction of suffering, our Lord endured this, also, to the uttermost, as the evangelists clearly show. You have read full often the story of His bod- ily sufferings. Take care that you never depreciate them; there was an amount of physical pain endured by our Savior which His body never could have borne unless it had been sustained and strengthened by union with His Godhead. Yet the sufferings of His soul were the soul of His sufferings. That soul of His endured a torment equivalent to hell itself; the punishment that was due to the wicked was that of hell, and though Christ suffered not hell, He suffered an equivalent of it. And now, can your minds conceive what that must have been? It was an anguish never to be measured, an agony never to be comprehended. It is to God, and God, alone, that His griefs were fully known. Well does the Greek liturgy put it, "Your unknown sufferings," for they must forever remain beyond guess of human imagination! See, brothers and sisters, Christ has gone thus far—He has taken the sin, taken the curse, and suffered the entire penal- ty; the last penalty of sin was death, and therefore the Redeemer died. Behold the mighty Conqueror yields up His life upon the tree; His side is pierced; the blood and water flows forth, and His disciples lay His body in the tomb. As He was first numbered with the transgressors, He was afterwards numbered with the dead. See, beloved, here is Christ bearing the curse instead of His people; here He is, coming under the load of their sin, and God does not spare Him, but smites Him as He must have struck us. He lays His full vengeance on Him. He launches all His thunderbolts against Him; He bids the curse wreak itself upon Him, and Christ suffers all, sustains all."

Charles Spurgeon: Christ Made A Curse For Us; Sermon 873 pgs. 5-6[90]

Now Christ has redeemed us from the curse of the Law, what are the blessings the saints have inherited?
    A) Christ paid the debut for me.
    B) Delivered from Hell.
    C) Saved from Gods wrath
    D) Given a New Creation nature
    E) Sealed by the Holy Spirit
    F) Given the Resurrection of Immortality and
        Eternal Life

90

G) Deliverance From All My Enemies
H) New Heavens and New Earth
I)   World without sin and death

Just in general the blessings of the Abrahamic Covenant are the redemption from all which Adam forfeited in the original fall in the Garden. First of all, what Jesus Christ did in becoming sin, and redeeming the saints from the curse has by the Blood of the Cross paid the debut to sin in full. Those who put their faith in Jesus Christ and confess Him as Lord and believe in their heart God has raised Him from the dead, you are saved.

Your debut to sin and death has been paid, Christ has in your behalf paid your debut to sin and Hell. Upon death you will go to Paradise, instead of Hell, and with the rest of the righteous dead will await your lot in resurrection of the righteous. Also, as your name is written in the Book of Life so you will be delivered from the Second death, the Lake of Fire and eternal torment.

Gods saints have not been appointed from wrath, and Gods wrath does not abide upon them like the rest of humanity who has not be saved through faith in Jesus Christ. Instead, you are born again with a new creation nature, a divine nature old things have died all things are become new. From the new nature in Christ, you are no longer a slave to sin, or under sins dominion.

In addition to a new nature, you have been given the Holy Spirit, by which you are sealed until the Day of

Redemption the resurrection of your soul and body into immortality. From the resurrection into immortality, you have received the right to be delivered from all your enemies including sin, Satan, and death. Which will be fully accomplished by Jesus Christ at the end of the Millennial Kingdom. At that time death, Hell, and Satan will be cast into the Lake of Fire, and the beginning of the New Heavens and New Earth world without sin will be your life. The Abrahamic Covenant and its promised redemption is beyond compare.

Chapter 12
Redeemed From Gods Wrath

One thing which has been difficult for the modern Church is to understand how Jesus Christ who died on the Cross is also the God who will come as the God of Sabaoth. The Lord of Host to who comes to make war in the Battle of Armageddon. Jesus Christ comes forth in robes of vengeance to make war with His enemies. Gods promised redemption includes His promise to execute His judgment upon all who refuse His way of redemption.

Isaiah 63:1-6[91]
1 Who is this that cometh from Edom, with dyed garments from Bozrah? this that is glorious in his apparel, travelling in the greatness of his strength? I that speak in righteousness, mighty to save.

---

[91]

2 Wherefore art thou red in thine apparel, and thy garments like him that treadeth in the winefat?
3 I have trodden the winepress alone; and of the people there was none with me: for I will tread them in mine anger and trample them in my fury; and their blood shall be sprinkled upon my garments, and I will stain all my raiment.
4 For the day of vengeance is in mine heart, and the year of my redeemed is come.
5 And I looked, and there was none to help; and I wondered that there was none to uphold: therefore, mine own arm brought salvation unto me; and my fury, it upheld me.
6 And I will tread down the people in mine anger, and make them drunk in my fury, and I will bring down their strength to the earth.

The Church must remember the foreshadowing of Gods wrath seen in the flood waters of Noah. The Scriptures warn before the Second Coming of Jesus Christ conditions on earth will be as in the Days of Noah. As violence filled the whole earth in the days of Noah, Jesus Christ warns of the same conditions in the last days. Wars and rumors of wars, kingdom against kingdom, and nations and tribes rising against one another in the last days.

The Scriptures also remind us the moral condition in the whole world will be like in the days of Sodom, at the time of Lot. The wrath of God rained down on Sodom, only Lot, Lots wife, and two daughters were delivered from the rain of fire. The apostle John in his visions of the Apocalypse say the bowls of Gods wrath pouring out burn the elements of the earth melting them in Gods wrath. The apostle Peter also confirms Gods wrath will be by fire upon creation, and upon fallen humanity.

The days of vengeance points to Gods curse, and finality of Gods wrath in this present evil age. The God who opened the windows of heaven to demonstrate His vengeance, His curse on sin, His wrath on a large scale also provided the way of escape for Noah and his family. Those who were hidden in the Ark were covered by Gods covenant of mercy. The deluge in the days of Noah was Gods curse poured out over the whole earth. None can declare the flood of Noah was anything, but the result of Gods curse, His wrath against sin. The rain fell out of heaven, the floodgates opened, the fountain of the deep until mankind was all judged unto death by the wrath of God.

Sodom and Gomorrah had given themselves to strange flesh, men with men, women with women, both young and old. From a place of safety Abraham lifted up his eyes to see the wrath of God reigning fire and brimstone out of heaven, Gods curse upon the sexually immoral Sodom. Finally, another example of Gods wrath exhibited as His curse is seen upon Satan himself. Once Lucifer, the chief of angels, now cursed by God cast out of heaven for a short season who end is Gods wrath.

God judged Satan to eternal flames which Satan will inhabit for all eternity in the Lake of Fire. What is the curse of God, the very essence of hell where the souls of the departed have been judged without hope, without mercy, without end? The end result of the curse of sin and death.

However, for the redeemed God has provided the way of escape. The righteous are not appointed for the wrath of God. The way of redemption has delivered them from Gods curse, and instead the saints have inherited the blessing given to Abraham. Indeed, Christ has redeemed us from the curse of the law, that the blessings of Abraham should come upon us by faith in Jesus Christ.

Romans 1:18-23[92]

18 For the wrath of God is revealed from heaven against all ungodliness and unrighteousness of men, who hold the truth in unrighteousness.

19 Because that which may be known of God is manifest in them; for God hath shewed it unto them.

20 For the invisible things of him from the creation of the world are clearly seen, being understood by the things that are made, even his eternal power and Godhead; so that they are without excuse:

21 Because that, when they knew God, they glorified him not as God, neither were thankful; but became vain in their imaginations, and their foolish heart was darkened.

92

22 Professing themselves to be wise, they became fools,
23 And changed the glory of the uncorruptible God into
an image made like to corruptible man, and to birds,
and four-footed beasts, and creeping things.

1 Thessalonians 5:1-9[93]
1 But of the times and the seasons, brethren, ye have
no need that I write unto you.
2 For yourselves know perfectly that the day of the Lord
so cometh as a thief in the night.
3 For when they shall say, Peace and safety; then
sudden destruction cometh upon them, as travail upon
a woman with child; and they shall not escape.
4 But ye, brethren, are not in darkness, that that day
should overtake you as a thief.
5 Ye are all the children of light, and the children of the
day: we are not of the night, nor of darkness.
6 Therefore let us not sleep, as do others; but let us
watch and be sober.
7 For they that sleep sleep in the night; and they that be
drunken are drunken in the night.
8 But let us, who are of the day, be sober, putting on
the breastplate of faith and love, and for a helmet, the
hope of salvation.
9 For God hath not appointed us to wrath, but to obtain
salvation by our Lord Jesus Christ,

93

Curse Over Creation

We have seen how God did not curse fallen man, instead cursed sin, and death. However, we do see how creation was cursed in the fall. Even creation itself has been corrupted by the curse of sin and death. In the end the corruption which is in creation will come into its heights.

Genesis 3:7-19[94]

17 And unto Adam he said, Because thou hast hearkened unto the voice of thy wife, and hast eaten of the tree, of which I commanded thee, saying, Thou shalt not eat of it: cursed is the ground for thy sake; in sorrow shalt thou eat of it all the days of thy life.
18 Thorns also and thistles shall it bring forth to thee; and thou shalt eat the herb of the field.
19 In the sweat of thy face shalt thou eat bread, till thou return unto the ground; for out of it wast thou taken: for dust thou art, and unto dust shalt thou return.

We can see Gods curse in the Garden extended to creation, as the curse of sin and death corrupted original creation. Now we see decay is the result of death, and the law of sin and death is exhibited in entropy. Instead of evolution where man and creation are evolving into perfection, the law of entropy says creation goes from a state of order to disorder. From order it goes into decay. Sometimes the process of entropy can be measured by time, the time it takes for

94

ordered things to grow old and decay. With original mankind it took longer from birth to death, sometimes men lived eight hundred to nine hundred years plus. The life span was much longer closer to the fall in the Garden. An example would be the life span of Adam was 930 years, before physical death even though the day Adam committed sin in the Garden he died spiritually.

After the flood of Noah, the life span of man was reduced significantly to what is ends up being today seventy years, and if by reason of strength eighty. Of course, men live over eighty years, but by that age they are significantly aged.
So, creation is groaning from the law of sin and death as defined by science as entropy. The nature of plants and animals was drastically altered when God cursed the ground stating the ground would produce thorns and thistles. That is what today is considered weeds in your garden. It is amazing how easily weeds grow, and on the other side of the coin how good crops need to be protected from weeds chocking them out. With fallen creation restored at the Second Coming of Jesus Christ, we see a change in plant and animal nature. A change from it predatory state of corruption to a kindlier creation able to dwell with other animals and humans.

Isaiah 11:3-9[95]

3 And shall make him of quick understanding in the fear of the Lord: and he shall not judge after the sight of his eyes, neither reprove after the hearing of his ears:
4 But with righteousness shall he judge the poor and reprove with equity for the meek of the earth: and he shall smite the earth with the rod of his mouth, and with the breath of his lips shall he slay the wicked.
5 And righteousness shall be the girdle of his loins, and faithfulness the girdle of his reins.
6 The wolf also shall dwell with the lamb, and the leopard shall lie down with the kid; and the calf and the young lion and the fatling together; and a little child shall lead them.
7 And the cow and the bear shall feed; their young ones shall lie down together: and the lion shall eat straw like the ox.
8 And the sucking child shall play on the hole of the asp, and the weaned child shall put his hand on the cockatrice' den.
9 They shall not hurt nor destroy in all my holy mountain: for the earth shall be full of the knowledge of the Lord, as the waters cover the sea.

Isaiah 65:25[96]

25 The wolf and the lamb shall feed together, and the lion shall eat straw like the bullock: and dust shall be the

---

95
96

serpent's meat. They shall not hurt nor destroy in all my holy mountain, saith the Lord.

With the Second Coming of the Lord the curse of sin and death will be finally broken. However, before then the earth's inhabitants will be destroyers of the earth, releasing wars and technology which will bring great devastation to the planet. Finally, God Himself will release catastrophic judgments in relationship to His Day of Vengeance acting upon those He has cursed.

Isaiah 24:1-6[97]
1 Behold, the Lord maketh the earth empty, and maketh it waste, and turneth it upside down, and scattereth abroad the inhabitants thereof.
2 And it shall be, as with the people, so with the priest; as with the servant, so with his master; as with the maid, so with her mistress; as with the buyer, so with the seller; as with the lender, so with the borrower; as with the taker of usury, so with the giver of usury to him.
3 The land shall be utterly emptied, and utterly spoiled: for the Lord hath spoken this word.
4 The earth mourneth and fadeth away, the world languisheth and fadeth away, the haughty people of the earth do languish.
5 The earth also is defiled under the inhabitants thereof; because they have transgressed the laws, changed the ordinance, broken the everlasting covenant.

6 Therefore hath the curse devoured the earth, and they that dwell therein are desolate: therefore, the inhabitants of the earth are burned, and few men left.

The prophet Isaiah saw thousands of years in advance Gods end time judgments and its effect on the whole world. Isaiah's prophetic words match with the visions which the apostle John saw in the Apocalypse concerning the wrath of God. The bowls of wrath poured out by Gods angels cause great catastrophic events both in the heaven and on earth. Even major portions of the earth's population will be destroyed with just one of the Bowls of God's Wrath.

Revelation 16:16-21[98]
16 And he gathered them together into a place called in the Hebrew tongue Armageddon.
17 And the seventh angel poured out his vial into the air; and there came a great voice out of the temple of heaven, from the throne, saying, It is done.
18 And there were voices, and thunders, and lightnings; and there was a great earthquake, such as was not since men were upon the earth, so mighty an earthquake, and so great.
19 And the great city was divided into three parts, and the cities of the nation's fell: and great Babylon came in remembrance before God, to give unto her the cup of the wine of the fierceness of his wrath.

98

20 And every island fled away, and the mountains were not found.
21 And there fell upon men a great hail out of heaven, every stone about the weight of a talent: and men blasphemed God because of the plague of the hail; for the plague thereof was exceeding great.

As God pours out His end time wrath millions or even billons of the earth's population will refuse to repent of their sins rejecting the way of salvation. They would rather to go into eternity under the wrath of God. In blasphemous hate of God are sent into Hell or the Lake of Fire instead of repenting to make it right with God. This proves the fallacy of Universal Salvation as men will refuse the mercy and grace of God even in the face of their own eternal damnation.

Revelation 9:18-21[99]
18 By these three was the third part of men killed, by the fire, and by the smoke, and by the brimstone, which issued out of their mouths.
19 For their power is in their mouth, and in their tails: for their tails were like unto serpents, and had heads, and with them they do hurt.
20 And the rest of the men which were not killed by these plagues yet repented not of the works of their hands, that they should not worship devils, and idols of gold, and silver, and brass, and stone, and of wood: which neither can see, nor hear, nor walk:

99

21 Neither repented they of their murders, nor of their sorceries, nor of their fornication, nor of their thefts.

Revelation 16:8-11
8 And the fourth angel poured out his vial upon the sun; and power was given unto him to scorch men with fire.
9 And men were scorched with great heat, and blasphemed the name of God, which hath power over these plagues: and they repented not to give him glory.
10 And the fifth angel poured out his vial upon the seat of the beast; and his kingdom was full of darkness; and they gnawed their tongues for pain,
11 And blasphemed the God of heaven because of their pains and their sores and repented not of their deeds.

When Does God Finally Lift the Curse

The final acts of Gods redemption will to put away all the effects of sin and death. As noted earlier this will require two ages. In the next age the curse of sin and death will be completely removed from all of creation. Right now, Gods plan of redemption gives fallen humanity the way of salvation providing forgiveness of sins, and the born-again experience. For all who confess Jesus Christ as Lord God gives the sealing of the Holy Spirit with the promise of the future resurrection of our mortal bodies.

At the end of this age is a time of Tribulation where the Judgments of God are finalized against the nations.

Catastrophic judgments which usher in the Second Coming of Jesus Christ, and the beginning of the Kingdom age. The start of the next age includes the first resurrection where the righteous dead in Christ are raised into immortality and are given the right to rule and reign with Jesus Christ for the one-thousand-year Kingdom Age. At the end of this age Satan is chained in the abyss, and evil spirits are judged placed into the eternal fire.

The kingdom age still has death, but men will die at a much older age. A man dying at one hundred will have considered to die young. So, death is still present at the beginning of the Millennial Kingdom, but by the end death and all its influence will be put under the feet of Jesus Christ. At the end of the Millennial age the covering of death and its curse all its corruption will finally be destroyed in all its capacity. Death will be no more neither will men die of sin as the Millennial Kingdom will be the time where deaths dominion is finally destroyed. As the Prophet Isaiah noted; death will be swallowed in victory, and the rebuke of the curse of sin and death shall the Lord take away from all the earth. Deaths face which has shadowed the whole earth cast over all peoples as a vail spread over the nations will be finally destroyed.
What the Lord has obtained by the incarnation, His death and resurrection, the Second Coming, and the Kingdom age now come to completion by destroying His

final enemy death. In the Kingdom age the curse of sin and death, and death itself are put away for all eternity.

Isaiah 25:7-9[100]
7 And he will destroy in this mountain the face of the covering cast over all people, and the vail that is spread over all nations.
8 He will swallow up death in victory; and the Lord God will wipe away tears from off all faces; and the rebuke of his people shall he take away from off all the earth: for the Lord hath spoken it.
9 And it shall be said in that day, Lo, this is our God; we have waited for him, and he will save us: this is the Lord; we have waited for him, we will be glad and rejoice in his salvation.

In its place will come the New heavens and New earth for the first heavens and earth corrupted by sin and death will have died. God will demonstrate the earth has been cleansed from sin and death, as the New Jerusalem the heavenly city will descend out of heaven upon the earth. The New Jerusalem will be Bridal in nature with all its citizens adorned as a Bride for her husband the Lord Jesus Christ. In this way the tabernacle of God will dwell with men, and God Himself shall be with them.

The conditions of sin and death will have died, God shall wipe all the tears of sorrow and pain from sin and death

---

100

away. No more sorrow, no more pain, no more sin, and no more death. For the former things which have resulted from the fall of man into sin, the curse of sin and death has all died.

The Lord who sits upon the Throne has become all in all; "behold I make all things new." Now the Lord has declared the beginning and end, the one who cursed sin and death, who drove man from the Garden from the Tree of Life now gives free access. I will give to Him who thirsts the fountain of life freely.

Revelation 21:1-8[101]
1 And I saw a new heaven and a new earth: for the first heaven and the first earth were passed away; and there was no more sea.
2 And I John saw the holy city, new Jerusalem, coming down from God out of heaven, prepared as a bride adorned for her husband.
3 And I heard a great voice out of heaven saying, Behold, the tabernacle of God is with men, and he will dwell with them, and they shall be his people, and God himself shall be with them, and be their God.
4 And God shall wipe away all tears from their eyes; and there shall be no more death, neither sorrow, nor crying, neither shall there be any more pain: for the former things are passed away.

---

[101]

5 And he that sat upon the throne said, Behold, I make all things new. And he said unto me, Write: for these words are true and faithful.
6 And he said unto me, It is done. I am Alpha and Omega, the beginning, and the end. I will give unto him that is athirst of the fountain of the water of life freely.
7 He that overcometh shall inherit all things; and I will be his God, and he shall be my son.
8 But the fearful, and unbelieving, and the abominable, and murderers, and whoremongers, and sorcerers, and idolaters, and all liars, shall have their part in the lake which burneth with fire and brimstone: which is the second death.

In the midst of the New Jerusalem, the heavenly city is found again the Tree of Life. The men who are now immortal saints can enter the city and partake of Christs life in fulness. Also, the river of Life clear as crystal which proceeds from the Throne of God. In the midst on either side of the river is the Tree of Life which gives fruit every month twelve manner of fruits, and healing for the nations. Gods people can partake freely, and without cost. It is life without the curse of sin and death. The Throne of God, and the Lamb shall be in it. God has achieved for all His saints the promised redemption, and sin and death are no more.

Revelation 22:1-3[102]
1 And he shewed me a pure river of water of life, clear
as crystal, proceeding out of the throne of God and of
the Lamb.
2 In the midst of the street of it, and on either side of
the river, was there the tree of life, which bare twelve
manner of fruits, and yielded her fruit every month: and
the leaves of the tree were for the healing of the
nations.
3 And there shall be no more curse: but the throne of
God and of the Lamb shall be in it; and his servants shall
serve him.

Conclusion
Do you love the Lord with all your heart? Do you seek
first the Kingdom living as a pilgrim, a sojourner on a
journey towards the Second Coming of the Lord? Have
you confessed Jesus Christ as the way God has made to
give you eternal life? Do you know as a Christian one set
apart by the Blood of Jesus Christ you will stand to give
an account for your works after coming into saving
faith? Do you make preparation for the coming of the
Lord? Love not the things of the world, but are looking
for a city whose builder and maker is God? Are you one
who will love the appearing of the Lord knowing as He is
so are, we in this present age?

Now those born of the Spirit through faith in Jesus
Christ are already sons of God. However, it does not yet

appear what we shall be, as we see in a glass (mirror) dimly but then face to face. For those who wholly follow the Lord there shall be no shame at his coming. For the high calling is to count all things loss in comparison of the excellence of gaining Christ. For all who are born of the Spirit who have the hope of being like Christ purifies himself even as he is pure. For the high calling to be part of the first resurrection called to the Marriage Supper of the Lamb is beyond anything this present world has to offer.

For eye has not seen, or has ear heard, or has entered into the heart of man, the things which God has prepared for those who love Him. For the Spirit and the Bride say, "Come Lord Jesus" If many man love not the Lord Jesus Christ, let him be Anathema Maranatha. Amen.

1 John 3:2-7[103]
2 Beloved now are we the sons of God, and it doth not yet appear what we shall be: but we know that, when he shall appear, we shall be like him; for we shall see him as he is.
3 And every man that hath this hope in him purifieth himself, even as he is pure.
4 Whosoever committeth sin transgresseth also the law: for sin is the transgression of the law.
5 And ye know that he was manifested to take away our sins; and in him is no sin.

103

6 Whosoever abideth in him sinneth not: whosoever sinneth hath not seen him, neither known him.
7 Little children let no man deceive you: he that doeth righteousness is righteous, even as he is righteous.

1 Corinthians 16:22-24[104]
22 If any man love not the Lord Jesus Christ, let him be Anathema Maranatha.
23 The grace of our Lord Jesus Christ be with you.
24 My love be with you all in Christ Jesus. Amen

Revelation 22:17-21
17 And the Spirit and the bride say, Come. And let him that heareth say, Come. And let him that is athirst come. And whosoever will, let him take the water of life freely.
18 For I testify unto every man that heareth the words of the prophecy of this book, if any man shall add unto these things, God shall add unto him the plagues that are written in this book:
19 And if any man shall take away from the words of the book of this prophecy, God shall take away his part out of the book of life, and out of the holy city, and from the things which are written in this book.
20 He which testifieth these things saith, Surely, I come quickly. Amen. Even so, come, Lord Jesus.
21 The grace of our Lord Jesus Christ be with you all. Amen.

104

Bibliography

1. Genesis 2:17
2. Romans 5:8-15
3. Revelation 20:11-15
4. Romans 3:9-18
5. Acts 2:22-32
6. Acts 2:24-32
7. 2 Peter 2:4-9
8. Wikipedia
9. Wikipedia
10. 1 Corinthians 3:10-15
11. Wikipedia
12. Festival icons for the Christian year by John Baggley 2000 ISBN 0-88141-201-5 pages 83-84
13. Justin. Dialogue with Trypho. Chapter 80).
14. Co-writer.com/heaven.htm
15. Romans 8:18-23
16. Revelation 20:1-6
17. Revelation 20:11-15
18. Philippians 3:8-15
19. GH Lang First Born Sons Their Rights and Risks; Chapter 8 The First Resurrection -A Prize, Paragraphs seven and eight
20. Luke 16:19-26
21. 2 Corinthians 5:1-9
22. John 3:13
23. Revelation 6:9-11
24. Romans 5:12-14

25. Ephesians 4:17-19
26. Ephesians 4:17-19
27. Ephesians 2:1-3
28. 1 John 3:4
29. 1 Corinthians 11:27-32
30. Ephesians 2:1-3
31. Ephesians 5:1-7
32. Wikipedia
33. Matthew 25:41-46
34. Revelation 20:1-3
35. Matthew 25:41
36. Luke 16:19-31
37. Revelation 14:9-11
38. Mark 9:41-48
39. Isaiah 66:22-24
40. Wikipedia
41. Wikipedia
42. Wikipedia
43. Wikipedia
44. John 3:14-21
45. John 3:18
46. Wikipedia
47. Romans 3:10-18
48. John 8:42-47
49. John 7:6-7
50. Psalm 9:17
51. Isaiah 5:14-16
52. Genesis 6:5-8

53. 2 Peter 2:4-9
54. 2 Peter 3:2-15
55. John 3:36
56. Romans 2:1-6
57. Romans 2:6-11
58. Romans 5:9
59. Jude 1:8-16
60. Hebrews 12:18-29
61. Hebrews 3:7-19
62. https://www.gotquestions.org/Gehenna.html [105]
63. Wikipedia
64. 1 Corinthians 3:11-15
65. Gospel of God, The (2 volume set), Chapter 24, by Watchman Nee
66. Matthew 7:21-23
67. 1 Corinthians 6:8-10
68. Ephesians 5:1-7
69. Galatians 5:19-21
70. Luke 12:36-48
71. Watchman Nee: The Gospel of God; Volume 2; Chapter 24 Section 10 0f 13
72. Collected Works of Watchman Nee, The (Set 1) Vol. 07: The Christian (5)
73. Matthew 7:21
74. Galatians 5:17-21
75. 2 Peter 1:4-11

---

76. Revelation 22:18-19

77. 2 Peter 2:1-3

78. Genesis 2:16-17

79. Deuteronomy 28:1-2

80. Deuteronomy 28:13-15

81. Genesis 3:13-15

82. Genesis 3:16-19

83. Genesis 3:21-24

84. Romans 7:7-13

85. Romans 8:3-4

86. Galatians 3:18-25

87. Deuteronomy 29:20-29

88.Galatians 3:6-14

89. Galatians 3:13-14

90. Charles Spurgeon: Christ Made A Curse For Us; Sermon 873 pgs. 5-6   91. Isaiah 63:1-6

92. Romans 1:18-23

93. 1 Thessalonians 5:1-9

94. Genesis 3:7-19

95. Isaiah 11:3-9

96. Isaiah 65:25

97. Isaiah 24:1-6

98. Revelation 16:16-21

99. Revelation 9:18-21

100. Isaiah 25:7-9

101. Revelation 21:1-8

102. Revelation 22:1-3

103. 1 John 3:2-7

104. 1 Corinthians 16:22-24

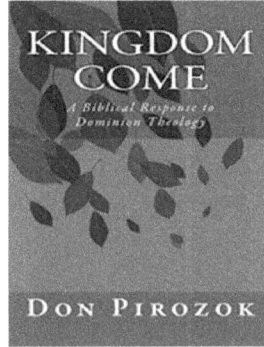

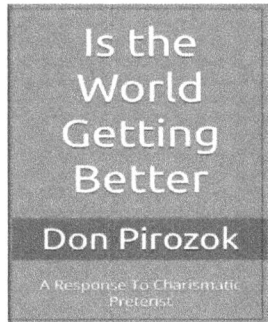

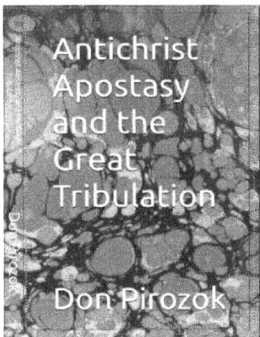

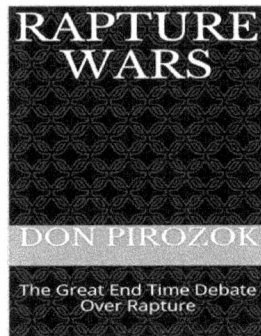

www.ingramcontent.com/pod-product-compliance
Lightning Source LLC
Chambersburg PA
CBHW061144040426
42445CB00013B/1534